Careers in Focus
MUSIC

Careers in Focus

MUSIC

Ferguson
An imprint of ☑ Facts On File

Ferguson
An imprint of Facts On File, Inc.
132 West 31st Street
New York NY 10001

Careers in focus. Music.
    p. cm.
Includes bibliographical references and index.
    ISBN 0-8160-5555-6 (alk. paper)
    1. Music—Vocational Guidance. I. J.G. Ferguson Publishing Company.
ML3795.C2793 2005
780'.23'73—dc22   2003003322

Ferguson books are available at special discounts when purchased in bulk quantities for businesses, associations, institutions, or sales promotions. Please call our Special Sales Department in New York at (212) 967-8800 or (800) 322-8755.

You can find Ferguson on the World Wide Web at http://www.fergpubco.com

Text design by David Strelecky

Printed in the United States of America

MP FOF 10 9 8 7 6 5 4 3 2 1

This book is printed on acid-free paper.

Table of Contents

Introduction

The music industry offers hundreds of fascinating and rewarding job opportunities for people with talent, drive, and ambition. Whether you are interested in writing, performing, teaching, or conducting music; producing, directing, or editing a music video; organizing Bach and Brahms scores and publications in a music library; helping a scared child through a medical test using music therapy; repairing broken clarinets and trombones in a music instrument repair shop; or booking or scouting musical talent at a popular jazz club, there is a career for you in the music industry.

This book describes a variety of careers in the music industry: in record companies, radio and television stations, libraries, publishing companies, concert halls and other performance venues, colleges and universities, health care settings, repair shops, and business offices. These careers are as diverse in nature as they are in their earnings and educational requirements. Earnings range from as little as $25 a night for an up-and-coming rock band to more than $1 million for well-known music video directors and top musicians. Many of these careers—such as musician, songwriter, and composer—require more artistic ability and sheer talent than formal education. Others—such as music teacher, music librarian, and music therapist—require a minimum of a bachelor's degree and sometimes even an advanced degree to enter the field.

The U.S. Department of Labor predicts strong growth for most music-related careers, but because so many young people want to work in this field, competition is intense. Although extremely talented workers have the best chances for success, the music industry holds no guarantees, even those with superior ability and talent. Many good musicians and other aspiring music industry professionals have second jobs waiting tables or filing in an office to make ends meet. In addition to musical ability and know-how, people skills, business knowledge, and a knack for self-promotion have become more and more important in this dynamic, growing industry.

The articles in this book appear in Ferguson's *Encyclopedia of Careers and Vocational Guidance,* but have been updated and revised with the latest information from the U.S. Department of Labor, professional organizations, and other sources. In addition, the following new articles have been written specifically for this book: Music Agents and Scouts, Music Journalists, Music Librarians, Music

Teachers, Music Therapists, Music Venue Owners and Managers, Music Video Directors and Producers, and Music Video Editors.

Each career article is divided into a number of sections. The **Quick Facts** section provides a brief summary of the career including recommended school subjects, personal skills, work environment, minimum educational requirements, salary ranges, certification or licensing requirements, and employment outlook. This section also provides acronyms and identification numbers for the following government classification indexes: the *Dictionary of Occupational Titles* (DOT), the *Guide for Occupational Exploration* (GOE), the National Occupational Classification (NOC) Index, and the Occupational Information Network (O*NET)-Standard Occupational Classification System (SOC) index. The DOT, GOE, and O*NET-SOC indexes have been created by the U.S. government; the NOC index is Canada's career-classification system. Readers can use the identification numbers listed in the Quick Facts section to access further information about a career. Print editions of the DOT (*Dictionary of Occupational Titles*. Indianapolis, Ind.: JIST Works, 1991) and GOE (*The Complete Guide for Occupational Exploration*. Indianapolis, Ind.: JIST Works, 1993) are available at libraries. Electronic versions of the NOC (http://www23.hrdc-drhc.gc.ca) and O*NET-SOC (http://online. onetcenter.org) are available on the World Wide Web. When no DOT, GOE, NOC, or O*NET-SOC numbers are present, this means that the U.S. Department of Labor or Human Resources Development Canada have not created a numerical designation for this career. In this instance, you will see the acronym "N/A," or not available.

The **Overview** section is a brief introductory description of the duties and responsibilities involved in this career. If a career may have a variety of job titles, alternative career titles are presented in this section.

The **History** section describes the history of the particular job as it relates to the overall development of its industry or field.

The Job describes the primary and secondary duties of the job.

Requirements discusses high school and postsecondary education and training requirements, any certification or licensing that is necessary, and other personal requirements for success in the job.

Exploring offers suggestions on how to gain experience in or knowledge of the particular job before making a firm educational and financial commitment. The focus is on what can be done while still in high school (or in the early years of college) to gain a better understanding of the job.

The **Employers** section gives an overview of typical places of employment for the job.

Starting Out discusses the best ways to land that first job, be it through the college placement office, newspaper ads, or personal contact.

The **Advancement** section describes what kind of career path to expect from the job and how to get there.

Earnings lists salary ranges and describes the typical fringe benefits.

The **Work Environment** section describes the typical surroundings and conditions of employment—whether indoors or outdoors, noisy or quiet, social or independent. Also discussed are typical hours worked, any seasonal fluctuations, and the stresses and strains of the job.

The **Outlook** section summarizes the job in terms of the general economy and industry projections. For the most part, Outlook information is obtained from the Bureau of Labor Statistics and is supplemented by information taken from professional associations. Job growth terms follow those used in the *Occupational Outlook Handbook*. Growth described as "much faster than the average" means an increase of 36 percent or more. Growth described as "faster than the average" means an increase of 21–35 percent. Growth described as "about as fast as the average" means an increase of 10–20 percent. Growth described as "more slowly than the average" means an increase of 3–9 percent. Growth described as "little or no change" means an increase of 0–2 percent. "Decline" means a decrease of 1 percent or more.

Each article ends with **For More Information**, which lists organizations that provide career information on training, education, internships, scholarships, and job placement.

Careers in Focus: Music also includes photos, informative sidebars, and interviews with professionals in the field.

If you have a passion for music and a strong desire to succeed, you could have a successful future in the music industry. Read about the variety of careers available in this exciting field, and be sure to contact the organizations listed for more information.

Artist and Repertoire Workers

OVERVIEW

In the artist and repertoire (A&R) department of a record company, *A&R coordinators, executives,* and other workers locate new talent and convince the company to sign them to contracts. A&R workers are also involved in producing their artists' CDs, promoting them, arranging concert tours, and other management details.

HISTORY

Talent scouts first became important to the recording industry in the 1950s, when pop and rock artists dominated the radio. For the first time in the country's history, teenagers were taken seriously as a consumer group, and their musical preferences made the small, independent companies that produced rock-and-roll records hugely successful. In the 1960s, record companies employed people who would match the professional musicians (artists) with songs (repertoire) written by professional composers. After a period of poor sales in the 1970s, record companies bounced back in the 1980s with the advent of the music video, which provided a whole new and profitable medium for marketing records. During this new era of big music business, A&R executives became even more powerful in the entertainment industry. Record companies relied on A&R professionals to sign and promote artists who had potential for quick, huge sales. Though record companies increasingly rely on major, break-out performers to generate large profits, A&R workers are still needed to develop a diverse group of artists that can bring their companies stable long-term returns on their investment.

THE JOB

Countless new bands emerge every year. For relatively unknown bands, gaining exposure through local, paying gigs can be very difficult. Trying to market a band nationally in an effort to get a record contract is even more difficult. A&R workers have firsthand knowledge of the number of artists hoping to sign with a record label—thousands of submissions cross their desks every year. A&R workers review these submissions for their record company, looking and listening for talented musicians. They listen to demo tape after demo tape, and read through press clippings and artist biographies. They also keep track of the music scene by attending clubs and reading fanzines. A&R workers visit websites and download samples. Although they listen to a lot of music that doesn't interest them, occasionally they come across something that stands out. When this happens, A&R workers set out to get to know the artist better. Just because A&R workers like an artist's demo tape doesn't mean they will automatically sign the artist

Listening Trends

Genre	Percent of U.S. Music Buyers Who Purchased Genre in 2002
Rock	24.7 percent
Rap/Hip-Hop	13.8 percent
R&B/Urban	11.2 percent
Country	10.7 percent
Pop	9.0 percent
Religious	6.7 percent
Jazz	3.2 percent
Classical	3.1 percent
Soundtracks	1.1 percent
Oldies	0.9 percent
New Age	0.5 percent
Children's	0.4 percent
Other	8.1 percent

Source: Recording Industry Association of America

to a contract. They first have to get a complete sense of the artist's talents. They may request additional recorded songs and attend live performances. Once they feel confident about the artist's talent, A&R workers attempt to get the artist a record deal. This involves convincing executives at the record company that the artist is worth the risk. But an A&R worker may also work with an artist that is being pursued by A&R representatives from other companies. In such cases, the A&R worker has to convince the artist that he or she will receive the attention and care he or she needs.

The work of A&R representatives doesn't end when they've signed the talent to a contract. A&R workers are closely involved in the careers of their artists. They help match them with producers and assist in the mixing of the tracks. They also help promote the artists—from helping them select the right clothes to wear for the CD cover photograph, to arranging interviews, to deciding which singles should be played on the radio. In order to guarantee that their investment is a profitable one, A&R representatives help their artists remain successful as performers and business people.

REQUIREMENTS

High School
Most A&R workers have a college degree, so in high school you should pursue a college-preparatory track. Classes in business, mathematics, speech, and English will be helpful. The most important thing you can do is to become involved in music, be it playing in a school band or with a group of friends, or simply listening to and becoming knowledgeable about a wide variety of music.

Postsecondary Training
Executives in the music industry come from a variety of backgrounds. You'll likely need a college degree, but experience with a record company will be the most valuable training. Some A&R workers have degrees in communications, business, marketing, and music.

Other Requirements
As an A&R worker, you'll need a love for music and an interest in the business end of the music industry. You should have a good sense of the history of popular music as well as the acts that are currently popular. You'll also need to be very organized; A&R workers for big companies generally must handle many different acts in different stages of production.

EXPLORING

Listen to a wide variety of music and follow the careers of your favorite recording artists by reading magazines and surfing the Internet. Listen especially to new talent as it emerges. There are certain radio stations that frequently feature new musicians. Visit clubs that regularly book live music.

Study music, including music performance and music history. If possible, join a group to learn about the challenges of performing with others, composing original music, booking gigs, and managing the business side of music.

EMPLOYERS

There are hundreds of record companies across the country, but many are small, independent labels staffed by very few people. Five corporations—Universal, Warner, Sony, BMG, and EMI—now control 80 percent of the recording industry in the United States and employ the majority of A&R workers. Major record labels include A&M, Geffen, MCA, Warner Bros., Atlantic, Columbia, Arista, Virgin, and Capitol. Most positions are located in Los Angeles, New York City, and Nashville.

STARTING OUT

Getting a job in A&R can be very difficult—such positions are highly sought after. Some major record companies offer internship opportunities; check with your college's internship office for information. After college, you can pursue an entry-level position with a record company. You should work in any department in which there's a job opening. Check the help wanted ads in such trade magazines as *Billboard* (http://www.billboard.com) and *Variety* (http://www.variety.com), or look for temporary employment agencies that specialize in placing people in jobs in the entertainment industry.

ADVANCEMENT

Once A&R workers gain some experience in the music industry, whether within a company, or as a freelance producer or manager, they will be able to make connections with other, more experienced A&R professionals. An A&R worker may begin as an assistant, then work up into a position as a coordinator, and later as a vice president or president of the department.

EARNINGS

A&R workers in entry-level positions make around $20,000 a year. More senior positions can pay upwards of $85,000. Experienced executives with major record companies can make more than $200,000 a year. Full-time employment with a record company usually includes health and retirement benefits, as well as bonuses.

WORK ENVIRONMENT

Work with a record company can be very exciting—A&R workers have the opportunity to make decisions about what music people will be listening to and which artists will get a shot at success. But the work can be very stressful and intense. A&R professionals work long hours, making phone calls, devising schedules, reviewing contracts, and handling many other details of management. They have to sort through a lot of bad music to find the few artists that interest them. They also devote many evenings to scouting out new talent at clubs.

OUTLOOK

The A&R worker will always be important to record companies, and positions within an A&R department will always be difficult to get. The work itself will be affected greatly by the Internet in the years to come. A&R workers surf the Web for artists who market themselves with their own websites. Technological advances have allowed for quick and easy music downloads, and some artists are now using the Web to bypass record companies entirely. So, in addition to competing with other record companies for talent, A&R workers may be competing with the artists themselves for the opportunity to distribute their music.

FOR MORE INFORMATION

Visit the NARAS website for information on the recording industry and for links to many music and recording-related sites.

National Academy of Recording Arts & Sciences (NARAS)
3402 Pico Boulevard
Santa Monica, CA 90405
Tel: 310-392-3777
http://grammy.com

For facts and statistics about the recording industry, contact
Recording Industry Association of America
1330 Connecticut Avenue, NW, Suite 300
Washington, DC 20036
Tel: 202-775-0101
http://www.riaa.com

For industry information, contact
The Society of Professional Audio Recording Services
PO Box 770845
Memphis, TN 38177
Tel: 800-771-7727
http://www.spars.com

Audio Recording Engineers

QUICK FACTS

School Subjects
Computer science
Music

Personal Skills
Mechanical/manipulative
Technical/scientific

Work Environment
Primarily indoors
Primarily one location

Minimum Education Level
Some postsecondary training

Salary Range
$18,540 to $36,970 to
$82,510+

Certification or Licensing
Recommended

Outlook
About as fast as the average

DOT
194

GOE
05.10.05

NOC
5225

O*NET-SOC
27-4011.00, 27-4012.00,
27-4014.00

OVERVIEW

Audio recording engineers oversee the technical end of recording. They operate the controls of the recording equipment—often under the direction of a music producer—during the production of music recordings; film, television, and radio productions; and other mediums that require sound recording. Recording engineers monitor and operate electronic and computer consoles to make necessary adjustments, and they solve technical problems as they occur during a recording session. They assure that the equipment is in optimal working order and obtain any additional equipment necessary for the recording.

HISTORY

The job of the contemporary audio recording engineer as we know it began in the late 1940s with the development of magnetic tape as a recording medium. Tape provided a new and flexible method of enabling recording engineers to influence the outcome of the recording session. Before tape, records were cut on warm wax blanks that allowed only minimal manipulation of sound quality. Generally, whatever the musicians produced in the recording studio is what came out on the record, and the degree of quality rested almost entirely in the hands of the studio engineer.

The innovation of tape and the introduction of long-playing (LP) records brought significant improvements to the recording industry. Since tape allowed for recording on multiple tracks, recording engineers were needed to edit and enhance tape quality and "mix" each track individually to produce a balanced sound on all tracks. Tape allowed recording engineers to perform patchwork corrections to a recording by replacing sections where musician errors or poor sound quality occurred.

By the 1950s recording engineers played a vital role in the record industry. The emergence of rock and roll brought an explosion of recordings in the industry, and each recording required a technically proficient, creative, and skilled audio recording engineer. Although engineers often had to produce sounds at the direction of the music producer, many worked at their own discretion and produced truly unique "sounds." Engineers also found employment for film productions in Hollywood and for radio station productions throughout the United States.

The development of music-related software for the computer has altered many aspects of music recording, particularly in the editing process. Many time-consuming tasks that were performed manually can now be done in half the time and less with new specially programmed software. More than ever before, today's audio recording engineer must be highly educated and up-to-date with the rapidly changing technology that ultimately affects the way he or she performs the job.

THE JOB

Audio recording engineers operate and maintain the equipment used in a sound recording studio. They record music, live and in studios; speech, such as dramatic readings of novels or radio advertisements; and sound effects and dialogue used in television and film. They work in control rooms at master console boards that often contain hundreds of dials, switches, meters, and lights, which the engineer reads and adjusts to achieve desired results during a recording. Today, the recording studio is often considered an extra instrument, thus the audio recording engineer becomes an extra musician in his or her ability to dramatically alter the final sound of the recording.

As the owner of Watchmen Studios in Lockport, New York, Doug White offers audio recording services, digital audio mastering, audio duplication, and Web page construction. "I record a lot of hardcore and metal," he says. "It makes up about 60 percent of what we do here." His clients include Bughouse, Big Hair, Tugboat Annie, and Slugfest. Watchmen Studios features separate drum, vocal, and guitar booths and offers 24-track, 16-track, and 8-track recording. The studio even offers spare guitars. "I try to keep it to a nine-hour day,"

White says. "Some studio engineers work up to 12 hours a day, but I feel my work suffers after too long."

As recording engineers prepare to record a session, they ask the musicians and producer what style of music they will be playing and what type of sound and emotion they want reflected in the final recording. Audio recording engineers must find out what types of instruments and orchestration will be recorded to determine how to manage the recording session and what additional equipment will be needed. For example, each instrument or vocalist may require a special microphone. The recording of dialogue will take considerably less preparation.

Before the recording session, audio recording engineers test all microphones, chords, recording equipment, and amplifiers to ensure everything is operating correctly. They load tape players and set recording levels. Microphones must be positioned in precise locations near the instrument or amplifier. They experiment with several different positions of the microphone and listen in the control room for the best sound. Depending on the size of the studio and the number of musicians or vocalists, audio recording engineers position musicians in various arrangements to obtain the best sound for the production. For smaller projects, such as three- to eight-piece bands, each instrument may be sectioned off in soundproof rooms to ensure the sounds of one instrument do not "bleed" into the recording of another instrument. For more complex recordings of larger orchestrations, specialized microphones must be placed in exact locations to record one or several instruments.

Once audio recording engineers have the musicians in place and the microphones set, they instruct musicians to play a sample of their music. At the main console, they read the gauges and set recording levels for each instrument. Recording engineers must listen for sound imperfections, such as hissing, popping, "mike bleeding," and any other extraneous noises, and pinpoint their source. They turn console dials to adjust recording level, volume, tone, and effects. Depending on the problem, they may have to reposition either the microphone or the musician.

With the right sound and recording level of each microphone set, audio recording engineers prepare the recording equipment (either tape or digital). During the recording of a song or voice-over, they monitor the recording level of each microphone to ensure none of the tracks are too high, which results in distortion, or too low, which results in weak sound quality. Recording engineers usually record more than one take of a song. Before the mixing process, they listen to each take carefully and determine which one has the best sound. They often splice the best part of one take with the best part of another take.

In some recording sessions, two engineers work in the control room. One usually works with the recording equipment, and the other takes instruction from the producer. The engineers implement the ideas of the producer to create the desired sound. During each session, the volume, speed, intensity, and tone quality must be carefully monitored. Producers may delegate more responsibility to the recording engineer. Engineers often tell the musicians when to start and stop playing or when to redo a certain section. They may ask musicians or other studio technicians to move microphones or other equipment in the studio to improve sound quality.

After the recording is made, the individual tracks must be "mixed" to a master tape. When mixing, they balance each instrument in relation to the others. Together with the producer and the musicians, recording engineers listen to the song or piece several times with the instruments at different levels and decide on the best sound and consistency. At this stage, they also set equalization and manipulate sound, tone, intensity, effects, and speed of the recording. Mixing a record is often a tedious, time-consuming task that can take several weeks to complete, especially with some recordings that are 24 or more tracks. At a larger studio, this may be done exclusively by a *sound mixer*. Sound mixers exclusively study various mixing methodologies.

Audio recording engineers frequently perform maintenance and repair on their equipment. They must identify and solve common technical problems in the studio. They may have to rewire or move equipment when updating the studio with new equipment. They may write proposals for equipment purchases and studio design changes. Apprentices, who are also known as *studio technicians,* often assist engineers in many of the basic sound recording tasks.

Recording engineers at smaller studios may set studio times for musicians. They must keep a thorough account of the band or performer scheduled to play, the musical style of the band or performer, the specific equipment that will be needed, and any other special arrangements needed to make the session run smoothly. They make sure the studio is stocked with the right working accessory equipment, including chords, cables, microphones, amplifiers, tapes, tuners, and effect pedals.

REQUIREMENTS
High School
You should take music courses to learn an instrument, study voice, or learn composition. High school orchestras and bands are an excellent source for both practicing and studying music performance. You

should also take classes in computer sciences, mathematics, business, and, if offered, electronics. A drama or broadcast journalism class may allow you access to a sound booth, and the opportunity to assist with audio engineering for live theatrical productions and radio programs.

Postsecondary Training

More than ever before, postsecondary training is an essential step for becoming a successful recording engineer. This is when you will make your first contacts and be introduced to many of the highly technical (and continually changing) aspects of the field. To learn about educational opportunities in the United States and abroad, visit the websites of the Audio Engineering Society (http://www.aes.org) or *Mix* online (http://mixonline.com).

Seminars and workshops offer the most basic level of education. This may be the best way to obtain an early, hands-on understanding of audio recording and prepare for entry-level apprentice positions. These programs are intended to introduce students to the equipment and technical aspects of the field, such as microphones, sound reinforcement, audio processing devices, tape and DAT machines, digital processing, and sound editing. Students will also become familiar with the newest technologies in the audio field, such as MIDI (musical instrument digital interface), synthesis, sampling, and current music software. A seminar can last from a couple of hours to several weeks. Many workshops are geared toward in-depth study of a certain aspect of recording such as mixing, editing, or music production.

Students looking for a more comprehensive course of study in specific areas of the recording industry can enroll in technical school or community college programs. Depending on the curriculum, these programs can take from several weeks to up to a year to complete. The most complete level of postsecondary education is a two- or four-year degree from a university. At many universities, students have access to state-of-the-art equipment and a teaching staff of knowledgeable professionals in the industry. Universities incorporate music, music technology, and music business in a comprehensive curriculum that prepares graduates to be highly competitive in the industry. Students can enroll in other non-audio courses, such as business, communications, marketing, and computers.

Certification or Licensing

In the broadcast industry, engineers can be certified by the Society of Broadcast Engineers (http://www.sbe.org). Certification is recommended because this step shows your dedication to the field and your level of competence. After completing technical training and

An audio recording engineer oversees the master console board during a recording session. *(Photo Disc)*

meeting strict qualifications, you can also join the society as a member or associate member. Membership gives you access to educational seminars, conferences, and a weekly job line.

Other Requirements

Being a recording engineer requires both technical skills and communication skills. You must be patient, capable of working well with a variety of people, and possess the confidence to function in a leadership position. Excellent troubleshooting skills are essential for an audio recording engineer.

"A very powerful, outgoing personality is the number one qualification," Doug White says. "You're dealing every day with picky musicians who never will be happy with their work, so they look to you for verification." White emphasizes that engineers need an even temperament and endless patience. "You have to be able to handle all types of personalities with kid gloves," he says.

EXPLORING

One way to learn more about this field is to read publications that focus on audio recording. *Mix* online (http://mixonline.com) offers articles about education, technology, and production. Other publications that provide useful information on the industry and audio recording techniques include *Remix* (http://www.remixmag.com), *Pro Sound News* (http://www.prosoundnews.com), and *Broadcast Engineering* (http://www.broadcastengineering.com).

Any experience you can get working in or around music will provide excellent background for this field. You could take up an instrument in the school band or orchestra, or perform with your own band. You might also have the opportunity to work behind the scenes with a music group, serving as a business manager, helping to set up sound systems, or working as a technician in a school sound recording studio or radio station.

Write or call record companies or recording studios to get more information; local studios can usually be found in the classified telephone directory, and others can be located in the music trade magazines. The National Academy of Recording Arts & Sciences (the organization responsible for the Grammy Awards) is one source for information on the industry. Numerous books and music trade magazines that cover music production are available at bookstores and libraries.

Doug White recommends that prospective recording engineers make appointments to interview working sound professionals. "Even if you have to buy an hour of studio time to sit with them and talk," he says, "it's worth the cost. Ask as much about the personal/social side of working with artists. Don't be dazzled by the equipment. Believe me, it's a very small part of the job."

EMPLOYERS

Though most major recording studios are located in metropolitan areas such as New York and Los Angeles, many cities across the country have vibrant music scenes. Talented, skilled engineers will always be in demand, no matter the size of the recording studio. Recording engineers may be employed by a studio, or they may be self-employed, either contracting with studios or operating their own recording business. Engineers also work for broadcast companies, engineering sound for radio and TV programs. Some recording engineers work for video production companies and corporate media libraries, helping to create in-house company presentations and films.

STARTING OUT

After high school, seek experience as an intern or apprentice or begin postsecondary training in audio at a university or college or trade school. Because most professional recording studios and broadcasters prefer to offer apprenticeship positions to students who have some previous experience in audio, those who have completed some trade school courses may have better chances at landing jobs. Most university and college programs offer semester internship programs at professional recording studios as a way of earning credit. Professional trade associations also support internships for their members by either matching students with employers or funding internship expenses. Universities and trade schools also have job placement services for their graduates.

Before going into the business, Doug White got an associate's degree from the Art Institute of Atlanta. "But in this business," he says, "your education doesn't get you very far. Reputation and experience are usually what open doors."

Internships and apprenticeships play an important role in helping students establish personal connections. Students are often hired by the studios or stations with which they've interned or their employer can make recommendations for other job openings at a different studio. Employers will often post entry-level openings at universities or trade schools, but very seldom will they advertise in a newspaper.

Most audio engineers begin their career in small studios as studio technicians and have varied responsibilities, which may entail anything from running out to pick up dinner for the musicians during a recording session, to helping the recording engineer in the mixing process. Positions in radio will also serve as a good stepping-stone to a career in audio recording. Entry-level positions may be easier to come by at studios that specialize in educational recording and radio advertisements than at music recording studios.

ADVANCEMENT

Career advancement will depend upon an engineer's interests as well as on hard work and perseverance. They may advance to the higher paying, glamorous (yet high-pressure) position of music producer, either as an independent producer or working for a record label. Recording engineers may also advance to positions in the radio or television industries, which usually offer better pay than studio work. If engineers wish to stay in the field of audio recording, they can advance to managerial positions or choose to open their own recording studio.

The recording industry is continually changing in response to frequent technological breakthroughs. Recording engineers who adapt easily to such advances as digital recording and new computer software will have a better chance for success. Some recording engineers may team up with producers who work independently of the studio. They may form their own company, allowing for greater flexibility and higher salaries.

EARNINGS

According to the U.S. Department of Labor, the median income for sound engineering technicians was approximately $36,970 in 2002. At the low end of the scale, about 10 percent of these workers made less than $18,540. The highest paid 10 percent made $82,510 or more. Audio engineers in the broadcast industry often earn higher salaries than those in the music industry. Generally, those working at television stations earned more than those working at radio stations.

Benefits packages will vary from business to business. Audio recording engineers employed by a recording company or by a broadcast station receive health insurance and paid vacation time. Other benefits may include dental and eye care, life and disability insurance, and a pension plan.

WORK ENVIRONMENT

Recording studios can be comfortable places to work. They are usually air-conditioned because of the sensitivity of the equipment. They may be loud or cramped, however, especially during recording sessions where many people are working in a small space. The work is not particularly demanding physically (except when recording engineers must move equipment), but there may be related stress depending on the personalities of the producer and the performers. Audio recording engineers must be able to follow directions from producers and must often give directions. Their work must be quick and precise, and the engineer must be able to work as part of a team. Depending on the type of recording business, some engineers may be required to record off-site, at live concerts, for example, or other places where the recording is to take place. Engineers can usually come to work dressed however they wish.

Engineers must have patience when working with performers. For the engineer, there are often long periods of waiting while the musicians or performers work out problems and try to perfect parts of their songs. Engineers frequently have to record the same piece several times after mistakes have been made in the presentation. In addition, the mixing process itself can become tedious for many engineers—especially if they are not fond of the music. During the mix, engineers must listen to the same song over and over again to assure a proper balance of the musical tracks, and they often try various mixes.

Working hours depend on the job. Some studios are open at night or on the weekends to accommodate the schedules of musicians and performers. Other studios and recording companies only operate during normal business hours. Engineers work between 40 and 60 hours a week and may frequently put in 12-hour workdays. Album or compact disc recordings typically take 300–500 hours each to record. In contrast, educational or language cassette recordings take only about 100 hours.

OUTLOOK

Employment in this field is expected to grow about as fast as the average over the next several years, according to the U.S. Department of Labor. New computer technology (hardware and software) is rapidly changing the way many recording engineers perform their jobs, making the entire audio recording process easier. These technological advancements will negatively affect job prospects for entry-level studio technicians, whose more mundane recording tasks will increasingly be performed by computers.

However, computer technology that makes the recording process faster and easier will free up time in the studio—time that the studio managers can book with more recording sessions, which in turn may require a larger staff. As this technology becomes affordable, though, some performers, particularly rock or jazz groups, may choose to record themselves. With computers doing most of the grunt work and allowing complete control and manipulation of sound, some of these home recordings (also called low-fi recordings) can sound just as good as a studio recording for certain music genres. However, to take full advantage of digital and multimedia technology, musicians will continue to seek out the expertise of studio professionals.

FOR MORE INFORMATION

For information on graduate-level scholarships and audio recording schools and courses in the United States and abroad, contact

Audio Engineering Society
60 East 42nd Street, Room 2520
New York, NY 10165
Tel: 212-661-8528
http://www.aes.org

For facts and statistics about the recording industry, contact
Recording Industry Association of America
1330 Connecticut Avenue, NW, Suite 300
Washington, DC 20036
Tel: 202-775-0101
http://www.riaa.com

For information on membership, contact
Society of Professional Audio Recording Services
PO Box 770845
Memphis, TN 38177
Tel: 800-771-7727
http://www.spars.com

Broadcast Engineers

OVERVIEW

Broadcast engineers, also referred to as broadcast technicians, or broadcast operators, operate and maintain the electronic equipment used to record and transmit the audio for radio signals and the audio and visual images for television signals to the public. They may work in a broadcasting station or assist in broadcasting directly from an outside site as a field technician. Approximately 36,000 broadcast engineers work in the United States.

HISTORY

At the end of the 19th century, Guglielmo Marconi, an Italian engineer, successfully sent radio waves across a room in his home and helped launch the age of mass communication. Marconi quickly realized the potential for his experiments. By 1901 he had established the Marconi Wireless Company in England and the United States and soon after successfully transmitted radio signals across the Atlantic Ocean for the first time.

At first, radio signals were used to transmit information and for communicating between two points, but eventually the idea was developed that radio could be used for entertainment, and in 1919, the Radio Corporation of America, or RCA, was founded. Families everywhere gathered around their radios to listen to music, drama, comedy, and news programs. Radio became a commercial success, and radio technology advanced, creating the need for skilled engineers to operate the complicated electronic equipment.

In 1933, frequency modulation, or FM, was introduced; originally there had been only amplitude modulation, or AM. The introduction

QUICK FACTS

School Subjects
Computer science
Mathematics

Personal Skills
Mechanical/manipulative
Technical/scientific

Work Environment
Indoors and outdoors
Primarily multiple locations

Minimum Education Level
Some postsecondary training

Salary Range
$14,600 to $27,760 to $65,970+

Certification or Licensing
Recommended

Outlook
About as fast as the average

DOT
194

GOE
01.02.03

NOC
5224

O*NET-SOC
27-4011.00, 27-4012.00, 27-4014.00

of FM vastly improved the quality of radio broadcasting. At the same time, people were experimenting with higher frequency radio waves, and in 1939 at the World's Fair in New York City, RCA demonstrated television to the public for the first time.

The effect television had on changing mass communication was as dramatic as the advent of the radio. Technology continued to advance with the introduction of color imaging, which became widely available in 1953. The number of VHF and UHF channels continued to increase; in the 1970s cable television and subscription television became available, further increasing the amount and variety of programming. Continuing advances in broadcast technology ensure the need for trained engineers who understand and can maintain the highly technical equipment used in television and radio stations.

One of the recent changes in technology that affects broadcast engineers is the switch from analog to digital signals. These changes provide ongoing challenges for television stations.

THE JOB

Broadcast engineers are responsible for the transmission of radio and television programming, including live and recorded broadcasts. Broadcasts are usually transmitted directly from the station; however, engineers are capable of transmitting signals on location from specially designed, mobile equipment. The specific tasks of the broadcast engineer depend on the size of the television or radio station. In small stations, engineers have a wide variety of responsibilities. Larger stations are able to hire a greater number of engineers and specifically delegate responsibilities to each engineer. In both small and large stations, however, engineers are responsible for the operation, installation, and repair of the equipment.

The *chief engineer* in both radio and television is the head of the entire technical operation and must orchestrate the activities of all the technicians to ensure smooth programming. He or she is also responsible for the budget and must keep abreast of new broadcast communications technology.

Larger stations also have an *assistant chief engineer* who manages the daily activities of the technical crew, controls the maintenance of the electronic equipment, and ensures the performance standards of the station.

Maintenance technicians are directly responsible for the installation, adjustment, and repair of the electronic equipment.

Video technicians usually work in television stations to ensure the quality, brightness, and content of the visual images being recorded and broadcast. They are involved in several different aspects of broadcasting and videotaping television programs. Technicians who are mostly involved with broadcasting programs are often called *video-control technicians*. In live broadcasts using more than one camera, they operate electronic equipment that selects which picture goes to the transmitter for broadcast. They also monitor on-air programs to ensure good picture quality. Technicians mainly involved with taping programs are often called *videotape-recording technicians*. They record performances on videotape using video cameras and tape-recording equipment and then splice together separate scenes into a finished program; they can create special effects by manipulating recording and re-recording equipment. The introduction of robotic cameras, six-foot-tall cameras that stand on two legs, created a need for a new kind of technician called a *video-robo technician*. Video-robo technicians operate the cameras from a control room computer, using joysticks and a video panel to tilt and focus each camera. With the help of new technology, one person can now effectively perform the work of two or three camera operators. Engineers may work with producers, directors, and reporters to put together videotaped material from various sources. These include networks, mobile camera units, and studio productions. Depending on their employer, engineers may be involved in any number of activities related to editing videotapes into a complete program.

REQUIREMENTS
High School
Take as many classes as you can in mathematics, science, computers, and shop, especially electronics. Speech classes will help you hone your abilities to communicate ideas to others in an effective manner.

Postsecondary Training
Positions that are more advanced require a bachelor's degree in broadcast communications or a related field. To become a chief engineer, you should aim for a bachelor's degree in electronics or electrical engineering. Because field technicians also act as announcers on occasion, speech courses and experience as an announcer in a school radio station can be helpful. Seeking education beyond a bachelor's degree will further the possibilities for advancement, although it is not required.

Certification or Licensing
The Federal Communications Commission licenses and permits are no longer required of broadcast engineers. However, certification from the Society of Broadcast Engineers (SBE) is desirable, and certified

engineers consistently earn higher salaries than uncertified engineers. The SBE offers an education scholarship and accepts student members; members receive a newsletter and have access to their job line.

Other Requirements
Broadcast engineers must have both an aptitude for working with highly technical electronic and computer equipment and minute attention to detail to be successful in the field. You should enjoy both the technical and artistic aspects of working in the radio or television industry. You should also be able to communicate with a wide range of people with various levels of technical expertise.

EXPLORING

Reading association publications is an excellent way to learn more about broadcast engineering. Many of the associations listed at the end of this article offer newsletters and other publications to members—some even post back issues or selected articles on their websites. You might also consider reading *Broadcast Engineering* (http://www.broadcastengineering.com), a trade publication for broadcast engineers and technicians.

You need experience before beginning a career as a broadcast engineer, and volunteering at a local broadcasting station is an excellent way to get it. Many schools have clubs for persons interested in broadcasting. Such clubs sponsor trips to broadcasting facilities, schedule lectures, and provide a place where students can meet others with similar interests. Local television station technicians are usually willing to share their experiences with interested young people. They can be a helpful source of informal career guidance. School officials can arrange visits or tours. Tours will enable you to see engineers at work. Most colleges and universities also have radio and television stations where students can gain experience with broadcasting equipment.

Exposure to broadcasting technology also may be obtained through building and operating an amateur, or ham, radio and experimenting with electronic kits. Dexterity and an understanding of home-operated broadcasting equipment will aid in promoting success in education and work experience within the field of broadcasting.

EMPLOYERS

According to the Federal Communications Commission, there were 13,296 radio stations and 1,714 television stations in the United States in 2002. These stations might be independently operated or owned

Top Radio Markets

According to Arbitron, an organization that measures radio audiences across the country, the top radio markets by population (age 12 and over) in Fall 2003 were

1. New York
2. Los Angeles
3. Chicago
4. San Francisco
5. Dallas-Forth Worth
6. Philadelphia
7. Houston-Galveston
8. Washington, D.C.
9. Boston
10. Detroit

and operated by a network. Smaller stations in smaller cities are good starting places, but it is at the larger networks and stations in major cities where the higher salaries are found. Some broadcast engineers work outside of the radio and television industries, producing, for example, corporate employee training and sales programs.

STARTING OUT

In many towns and cities there are public-access cable television stations and public radio stations where high school students interested in broadcasting and broadcast technology can obtain an internship. An entry-level technician should be flexible about job location; most begin their careers at small stations and with experience may advance to larger-market stations.

ADVANCEMENT

Entry-level engineers deal exclusively with the operation and maintenance of their assigned equipment; in contrast, a more advanced broadcast engineer directs the activities of entry-level engineers and makes judgments on the quality, strength, and subject of the material being broadcast.

After several years of experience, a broadcast engineer may advance to assistant chief engineer. In this capacity, he or she may direct the daily activities of all of the broadcasting engineers in the station as well as the field engineers broadcasting on location. Advancement to chief engineer usually requires at least a college degree in engineering and many years of experience. A firm grasp of management skills, budget planning, and a thorough knowledge of all aspects of broadcast technology are necessary to become the chief engineer of a radio or television station.

EARNINGS

Larger stations usually pay higher wages than smaller stations, and television stations tend to pay more than radio stations. Also, commercial stations generally pay more than public broadcasting stations. The median annual earnings for broadcast technicians were $27,760 in 2002, according to the U.S. Department of Labor. The department also reported that the lowest paid 10 percent earned less than $14,600 and the highest paid 10 percent earned more than $65,970 during that same period. Experience, job location, and educational background are all factors that influence a person's pay.

WORK ENVIRONMENT

Most engineers work in a broadcasting station that is modern and comfortable. The hours can vary; because most broadcasting stations operate 24 hours a day, seven days a week, there are engineers who must work at night, on weekends, and on holidays. Transmitter technicians usually work behind the scenes with little public contact. They work closely with their equipment and as members of a small crew of experts whose closely coordinated efforts produce smooth-running programs. Constant attention to detail and having to make split-second decisions can cause tension. Since broadcasts also occur outside of the broadcasting station on location sites, field technicians may work anywhere and in all kinds of weather.

OUTLOOK

According to the U.S. Department of Labor, the overall employment of broadcast technicians is expected to grow about as fast as the average over the next several years. There will be strong competition for jobs in metropolitan areas. In addition, the U.S. Department of Labor predicts that a slow growth in the number of new radio and television stations may mean few new job opportunities in the field. Technicians trained in the installation of transmitters should have better work prospects as television stations switch from their old analog transmitters to digital transmitters. Job openings will also result from the need to replace existing engineers who often leave the industry for other jobs in electronics.

FOR MORE INFORMATION

For information on its summer internship program, contact
  Association of Local Television Stations
  1320 19th Street, NW, Suite 300
  Washington, DC 20036
  Tel: 202-887-1970
  http://www.altv.com

Visit the BEA website for useful information about broadcast education and the broadcasting industry.
  Broadcast Education Association (BEA)
  1771 N Street, NW
  Washington, DC 20036
  Tel: 888-380-7222
  http://www.beaweb.org

For broadcast education, support, and scholarship information, contact
  National Association of Broadcasters
  1771 N Street, NW
  Washington, DC 20036
  Tel: 202-429-5300
  http://www.nab.org

For information on union membership, contact
  National Association of Broadcast Employees and Technicians
  http://nabetcwa.org

For information on student membership, scholarships, and farm broadcasting, contact
  National Association of Farm Broadcasters
  PO Box 500
  700 Branch Street, Suite 8
  Platte City, MO 64079

Tel: 816-431-4032
http://nafb.com

For information on careers in the cable industry, visit the NCTA website.
National Cable & Telecommunications Association (NCTA)
1724 Massachusetts Avenue, NW
Washington, DC 20036
Tel: 202-775-3550
http://www.ncta.com

For scholarship and internship information, contact
Radio-Television News Directors Association & Foundation
1600 K Street, NW, Suite 700
Washington, DC 20006
Tel: 202-659-6510
http://www.rtnda.org

For information on membership, scholarships, and certification, contact
Society of Broadcast Engineers
9247 North Meridian Street, Suite 305
Indianapolis, IN 46260
Tel: 317-846-9000
http://www.sbe.org

Composers and Arrangers

OVERVIEW

Composers create much of the music heard every day on radio and television, in theaters and concert halls, on recordings and in advertising, and through any other medium of musical presentation. Composers write symphonies, concertos, and operas; scores for theater, television, and cinema; and music for musical theater, recording artists, and commercial advertising. They may combine elements of classical music with elements of popular musical styles such as rock, jazz, reggae, folk, and others. *Arrangers* take composers' musical compositions and transcribe them for other instruments or voices; work them into scores for film, theater, or television; or adapt them to styles that are different from the one in which the music was written.

HISTORY

Classical composition probably (in its broadest sense) dates back to the late Middle Ages, when musical notation began to develop in Christian monasteries. In those times and for some centuries thereafter, the church was the main patron of musical composition. During the 14th century, or possibly earlier, the writing of music in score (that is, for several instruments or instruments and voices) began to take place. This was the beginning of orchestral writing. Composers then were mostly sponsored by the church and were supposed to be religiously motivated in their work, which was not to be considered an expression of their own emotions. It was probably not until the end of the 15th century that

QUICK FACTS

School Subjects
Music
Theater/dance

Personal Skills
Artistic
Communication/ideas

Work Environment
Primarily indoors
Primarily one location

Minimum Education Level
High school diploma

Salary Range
$2,000 to $31,310 to
$1,000,000+

Certification or Licensing
None available

Outlook
About as fast as the average

DOT
152

GOE
01.04.02

NOC
5132

O*NET-SOC
27-2041.02, 27-2041.03

the work of a composer began to be recognized as a statement of individual expression. Recognition of composers did not really become common until several centuries later. Even Johann Sebastian Bach, writing in the 18th century, was known more as an organist and choirmaster than a composer during his lifetime.

The writing of music in score was the beginning of a great change in the history of music. The craft of making musical instruments and the techniques of playing them were also advancing. By the beginning of the baroque period, around 1600, these changes brought musical composition to a new stage of development, which was enhanced by patronage from secular sources. The nobility had taken an interest in sponsoring musical composition, and over the next two or three centuries they came to supplant the church as the main patrons of composers. Under their patronage, composers had more room to experiment and develop new musical styles.

Until the end of the baroque period in about 1750, there was a flowering of musical forms, including opera. In the early 1600s, Rome became preeminent in opera, using the chorus and dance to embellish the operatic spectacle. Instrumental music also grew during this period, reaching its greatest flowering in the work of Johann Sebastian Bach and George Frederick Handel. The major musical forms of baroque origin were the sonata and cantata, both largely attributed to the composers of opera.

The "true" classical period in music began in about the mid-18th century and lasted through the 19th century. Composers embellishing the sonata form now developed the symphony. Through the latter half of the 19th century, most composers of symphonies, concerti, chamber music, and other instrumental forms adhered to the strict formality of the classical tradition. In the 19th century, however, many composers broke from classical formalism, instilling greater emotionalism, subjectivity, and individualism in their work. The new musical style evolved into what became formally known as the Romantic movement in music. Romanticism did not replace classicism, but rather, it existed side by side with the older form. A transitional figure in the break from classicism was Ludwig van Beethoven, whose compositions elevated the symphonic form to its highest level. Other composers who perfected the Romantic style included Franz Schubert, Franz Liszt, Johannes Brahms, Hector Berlioz, and Peter Ilich Tchaikovsky in orchestral music, and Giuseppe Verdi and Richard Wagner in opera.

Many of the composers of the early classical period labored for little more than recognition. Their monetary rewards were often meager. In the 19th century, however, as the stature of the composers grew, they were able to gain more control over their own work and the proceeds that it produced. The opera composers, in particular, were able to reap quite handsome profits.

Another abrupt break from tradition occurred at the beginning of the 20th century. At that time composers began to turn away from Romanticism and seek new and original styles and sounds. Audiences sometimes were repulsed by these new musical sounds, but eventually they were accepted and imitated by other composers. One of the most successful of the post-Romantic composers was Igor Stravinsky, whose landmark work *The Rite of Spring* was hailed by some to be the greatest work of the century.

Through the 20th century composers continued to write music in the styles of the past and to experiment with new styles. Some contemporary composers, such as George Gershwin and Leonard Bernstein, wrote for both popular and serious audiences. John Cage, Philip Glass, Steve Reich, and other composers moved even further from traditional forms and musical instruments, experimenting with electronically created music, in which an electronic instrument, such as a synthesizer, is used to compose and play music. An even more significant advance is the use of computers as a compositional tool. In the 21st century, the only thing predictable in musical composition is that experimentation and change are certain to continue.

THE JOB

Composers express themselves in music much as writers express themselves with words, or painters with line, shape, and color. Composing is hard work. Although they are influenced by what they hear, composers' works are original because they reflect their own interpretation and use of musical elements. All composers use the same basic musical elements, including harmony, melody, counterpoint, and rhythm, but each composer applies these elements in a unique way. Music schools teach all of the elements that go into composition, providing composers with the tools needed for their work, but how a composer uses these tools to create music is what sets an individual apart.

There is no prescribed way for a composer to go about composing. All composers work in a somewhat different way, but generally speaking they pursue their work in some kind of regular, patterned way, in much the same fashion of a novelist or a painter. Composers may work in different areas of classical music, writing, for example, symphonies, operas, concerti, music for a specific instrument or grouping of instruments, and for voice. Many composers also work in popular music and incorporate popular music ideas in their classical compositions.

Composers may create compositions out of sheer inspiration, with or without a particular market in mind, or they may be commissioned to write a piece of music for a particular purpose. Composers who write music on their own then have the problem of finding someone to perform their music in the hopes that it will be well received and lead to further performances and possibly a recording. The more a composer's music is played and recorded, the greater the chances to sell future offerings and to receive commissions for new work. Commissions come from institutions (where the composer may or may not be a faculty member), from societies and associations, and orchestral groups, or from film, television, and commercial projects. Almost every film has a score, the music playing throughout the film apart from any songs that may also be in the film.

A composer who wishes to make a living by writing music should understand the musical marketplace as well as possible. It should be understood that only a small percentage of music composers can make their living solely by writing music. To make a dent in the marketplace one should be familiar with its major components:

Performance. Composers usually rely on having their music performed in one of two ways: They contact musical performers or producers who are most likely to be receptive to their style of composition, or they may write for a musical group in which they are performers.

Music publishing. Music publishers seek composers who are talented and whose work they feel will be profitable to promote. They take a cut of the royalties, but they relieve composers of all of the business and legal detail of their profession. Composers today often self-publish their works.

Copying. A musical composition written for several pieces or voices requires copying into various parts. Composers may do this work themselves, but it is an exacting task for which professional copiers may be employed. Many composers themselves take on copying work as a sideline.

Computerization. Computers have become an increasingly important tool for composing and copying. Some composers have set up incredibly sophisticated computerized studios in which they compose, score, and play an orchestrated piece by computer. They can also do the copying and produce a recording. Perhaps the most significant enhancement to the home studio is MIDI (musical instrument digital interface), which transposes the composer's work into computer language and then converts it into notation.

Recording. Knowing the recording industry is important to a composer's advancement. An unrecognized composer will find it difficult to catch on with a commercial recording company, but it is not uncommon for a composer to make his own recording and handle the distribution and promotion as well.

Film and television. There is a very large market for original compositions in feature and industrial films, television programs, and videos. The industry is in constant need of original scores and thematic music.

Students interested in composing can tap into any number of organizations and associations for more detail on any area of musical composition. One such organization providing support and information is Meet the Composer, which is headquartered in New York City and has several national affiliates.

Arrangers generally create a musical background for a preexisting melody. An arranger may create an introduction and a coda (ending) for a melody as well as add countermelodies (additional melodies) to the original melody. In effect, the arranger composes additional material that was not provided by the composer and ensures that the original melody is set off by its background in an effective manner. Most arrangers are musicians themselves and have an excellent knowledge of musical styles and current trends.

An *orchestrator* takes a piece of music, perhaps one that already has a basic arrangement, and assigns the parts to specific instruments in the orchestra or other ensemble. For this reason, the orchestrator must have a tremendous amount of knowledge regarding exactly what the various instruments can and cannot do. An orchestrator may decide, for example, that a particular melody should be played by a solo flute or by a flute and an oboe, so that a very specific sound will be achieved. An orchestrator must also know how to write parts for various instruments. All the choices that the orchestrator makes will have a significant impact on the way the music will sound. Arranging and orchestrating are very closely related, and many professionals perform both tasks. Many composers also do their own arranging and orchestrating.

REQUIREMENTS
High School
There is no specific course of training that will help you to become a composer. Many composers begin composing at a very early age and receive tutoring and training to encourage their talent. Musically inclined students should continue their private studies and take

advantage of everything musical their high school offers. Gifted students usually find their way to schools or academies that specialize in music or the arts. These students may begin learning composition in this special environment, and some might begin to create original compositions.

Postsecondary Training

After high school, you can continue your education in any of numerous colleges and universities or special music schools or conservatories that offer bachelor's and advanced degrees. Your course of study will include music history, music criticism, music theory, harmony, counterpoint, rhythm, melody, and ear training. In most major music schools courses in composition are offered along with orchestration and arranging. Courses are also taught covering voice and the major musical instruments, including keyboard, guitar, and, more recently, synthesizer. Most schools now cover computer techniques as applied to music as well. It is also helpful to learn at least one foreign language; German, French, and Italian are good choices.

Other Requirements

Attending a musical institution is not a requirement for becoming a composer, nor is it any guarantee of success. Some say that composing cannot be taught, that the combination of skills, talent, and inspiration required to create music is a highly individualized phenomenon. Authorities have argued on both sides of this issue without resolution. It does appear that genetics plays a strong part in musical ability: Musical people often come from musical families. There are many contradictions of this, however, and some authorities cite the musical environment as being highly influential. The great composers were extraordinarily gifted, and it is very possible that achieving even moderate success in music requires special talent. Nevertheless, you will not be successful unless you work extremely hard and remain dedicated to improving your compositional talents at every opportunity. Prospective composers are also advised to become proficient on at least one instrument.

EXPLORING

Musical programs at local schools, YMCAs, and community centers offer good beginning opportunities. It is especially helpful to learn to play a musical instrument, such as the piano, violin, or cello. Attending concerts and recitals and reading about music and musicians and their careers will also provide you with good background and experience. There are also many videos available through your school or local library that will teach you about music. You should also form or join musical groups and attempt to write music for your group to perform. There are also many books that serve as good references on careers in composing and arranging.

EMPLOYERS

Composers are self-employed. They complete their work in their own studios and then try to sell their pieces to music publishers, film and television production companies, or recording companies. Once their work becomes well known, clients, such as film and television producers, dance companies, or musical theater producers, may commission original pieces from composers. In this case, the client provides a story line, time period, mood, and other specifications the composer must honor in the creation of a musical score.

Advertising agencies and studios that make commercials and film, television, and video production studios might have a few "house" composers on staff. Schools often underwrite a composer in residence, and many composers work as professors in college and university music departments while continuing to compose. For the most part, however, composers are on their own when creating and promoting their work.

Most arrangers work on a freelance basis for record companies, musical artists, music publishers, and film and television production companies.

STARTING OUT

In school, young composers should try to have their work performed either at school concerts or by local school or community ensembles. This will also most likely involve the composers in copying and scoring their work and possibly even directing. Student film projects can provide an opportunity for experience at film composing and scoring. Working in school or local musical theater companies can provide valuable experience. Personal connections made through these projects may be very helpful in the professional world. Developing a portfolio of work will be helpful as the composer enters a professional career.

Producers of public service announcements, or PSAs, for radio and television are frequently on the lookout for pro bono (volunteer) work that can provide opportunities for young, willing composers. Such opportunities may be listed in trade magazines, such as *Variety* (available in print or online at http://www.variety.com) and *Show Business* (in print or online at http://showbusinessweekly.com).

Joining the American Federation of Musicians and other musical societies and associations is another good move for aspiring composers. Among the associations that can be contacted are Meet the Composer, the American Composers Alliance, Broadcast Music, Inc., the Society of Composers, and the American Society of Composers, Authors, and Publishers (ASCAP), all located in New York City. These associations and the trade papers are also good sources for leads on grants and awards for which composers can apply.

Young composers, arrangers, songwriters, and jingle writers can also work their way into the commercial advertising business by doing some research and taking entry-level jobs with agencies that handle commercials involving music.

ADVANCEMENT

The advancement path in the music-composition and arrangement world is very individualized. There is no hierarchical structure to climb, although in record companies a person with music writing talent might move into a producing or A&R (artist and repertoire) job and be able to exercise compositional skills in those capacities. Advancement is based on talent, determination, and luck. Some composers become well known for their work with film scores; John Williams, of *Star Wars* fame, is one example.

Advancement for composers and arrangers is dependent on talent and skill. They may progress through their careers to writing or transcribing music of greater complexity and in more challenging structures. They may develop a unique style and even develop new forms and traditions of music. One day, their names might be added to the list of the great composers and arrangers.

EARNINGS

A few composers make huge annual incomes, while many make little or nothing. Some make a very large income in one or two years and none in succeeding years. While many composers receive royalties on repeat performances of their work, most depend on commissions to support themselves. Commissions vary widely according to the type of work and the industry for which the work will be performed. The U.S. Department of Labor reports that the median yearly income for music directors, composers, and arrangers holding salaried positions was $31,310 in 2002. However, earnings range widely. The lowest paid 10 percent of this group made less than $14,590 in 2002, while the highest paid 10 percent earned more than $67,330.

Many composers, however, do not hold full-time salaried positions and are only paid in royalties for their compositions that sell. According to the ASCAP, the royalty rate for 2003 was $.08 per song per album sold. The $.08 is divided between the composer and the publisher, based on their agreement. Since 2003, the composer and publisher will now receive an additional $.005 per album sold. Therefore, given these royalty rates, a composer with one song on an album that sold 200,000 copies in 2003 would receive $16,000 to be divided with his or her publisher. If the album sold another 25,000 copies in 2004 the royalties the composer and publisher received would be $2,125. Naturally, if this song is the only one the composer has that brings in income during this time, his or her annual earnings are extremely low (keep in mind that the composer receives only a percentage of the $16,000 and the $2,125).

On the other hand, a composer who creates music for a feature film may have substantial earnings, according to the ASCAP. Factors that influence the composer's earnings include how much music is needed for the film, the film's total budget, if the film will be distributed to a general audience or have only limited showings, and the reputation of the composer. The ASCAP notes that depending on such factors, a composer can receive fees ranging from $20,000 for a lower budget, small film to more than $1 million if the film is a big-budget release from a major studio and the composer is well known.

Many composers and arrangers must hold a second job in order to make ends meet financially. In some cases these second jobs, such as teaching, will provide benefits such as health insurance and paid vacation time. Composers and arrangers who work independently, however, need to provide their own insurance and other benefits.

WORK ENVIRONMENT

The physical conditions of a composer's workplace can vary according to personal taste and what is affordable. Some work in expensive, state-of-the-art home studios, others in a bare room with an electric keyboard or a guitar. An aspiring composer may work in a cramped and cluttered room in a New York City tenement or in a Hollywood ranch home.

For the serious composer the work is likely to be personally rewarding but financially unrewarding. For the commercial writer, some degree of financial reward is more likely, but competition is fierce, and top earnings go only to the rarest of individuals. Getting started requires great dedication and sacrifice. Even those protected by academia must give up most of their spare time to composing, often sitting down to the piano when exhausted from a full day of teaching. There are many frustrations along the way. The career composer must learn to live with rejection and have the verve and determination to keep coming back time and again. Under these circumstances, composers can only succeed by having complete faith in their own work.

OUTLOOK

The U.S. Department of Labor, which classifies composers and arrangers in the category of musicians, singers, and related workers, predicts employment in this field to grow about as fast as the average over the next several years. Although there are no reliable statistics on the number of people who make their living solely from composing and/or arranging, the general consensus is that very few people can sustain themselves through composing and arranging alone. The field is highly competitive and crowded with highly talented people trying to have their music published and played. There are only a limited number of commissions, grants, and awards available at any time, and the availability of these is often subjected to changes in the economy. On the other hand, many films continue to be made each year, particularly as cable television companies produce more and more original programs. However, the chances of new composers and arrangers supporting themselves by their music alone will likely always remain small.

FOR MORE INFORMATION

For profiles of composers of concert music, visit the ACA website.
   American Composers Alliance (ACA)
   73 Spring Street, Room 505
   New York, NY 10012
   Tel: 212-362-8900
   http://www.composers.com

For professional and artistic development resources, contact
   American Composers Forum
   332 Minnesota Street, Suite East 145
   St. Paul, MN 55101-1300
   Tel: 651-228-1407
   http://www.composersforum.org

For music news, news on legislation affecting musicians, and the magazine International Musician, contact
American Federation of Musicians of the United States and Canada
1501 Broadway, Suite 600
New York, NY 10036
Tel: 212-869-1330
http://www.afm.org

For articles on songwriting, information on workshops and awards, and practical information about the business of music, contact
American Society of Composers, Authors, and Publishers
One Lincoln Plaza
New York, NY 10023
Tel: 800-95-ASCAP
http://www.ascap.com

This organization represents songwriters, composers, and music publishers. Its website has useful information on the industry.
Broadcast Music, Inc.
320 West 57th Street
New York, NY 10019
Tel: 212-586-2000
http://www.bmi.com

The IAWM website has information for and about women composers.
International Alliance for Women in Music (IAWM)
Department of Music
422 South 11th Street, Room 209
Indiana University of Pennsylvania
Indiana, PA 15705
Tel: 724-357-7918
http://music.acu.edu/www/iawm

The Meet the Composer website has information on awards and residencies as well as interviews with composers active in the field today.
Meet the Composer
75 Ninth Avenue, 3R Suite C
New York, NY 10011
Tel: 212-645-6949
http://www.meetthecomposer.org

For information on student membership and commission competitions, contact
Society of Composers
Old Chelsea State
Box 450
New York, NY 10113
http://www.societyofcomposers.org

The SGA offers song critiques and other workshops in select cities. Visit its website for further information on such events and answers to frequently asked questions about becoming a songwriter.
Songwriters Guild of America (SGA)
1222 16th Avenue South, Suite 25
Nashville, TN 37212
Tel: 615-329-1782
http://www.songwriters.org

Disc Jockeys

OVERVIEW

Disc jockeys (DJs) play recorded music for radio stations or for parties, dances, and special events. On the radio, they intersperse the music with a variety of advertising material and informal commentary. They may also perform such public services as announcing the time, the weather forecast, travel times, or important news. Interviewing guests and making public service announcements may also be part of the DJ's work.

HISTORY

Guglielmo Marconi, a young Italian engineer, first transmitted a radio signal in his home in 1895. Radio developed rapidly as people began to comprehend its tremendous possibilities. The stations KDKA in Pittsburgh and WWWJ in Detroit began broadcasting in 1920. Within 10 years, there were radio stations in all the major cities in the United States and broadcasting had become big business. The National Broadcasting Company became the first network in 1926 when it linked together 25 stations across the country. The Columbia Broadcasting System was organized the following year. In 1934, the Mutual Broadcasting Company was founded. The years between 1930 and 1950 may be considered the zenith years for the radio industry. With the coming of television, radio broadcasting took second place in importance as entertainment for the home, but radio's commercial and communications value should not be underestimated.

The first major contemporary disc jockey in the United States was Alan Freed, who worked in the 1950s on WINS radio in New York. In 1957, his rock-and-roll stage shows at the Paramount Theater made front-page news in the *New York Times* because of the huge crowds they attracted. The title *disc jockey* arose when most music was recorded on conventional flat records or discs.

Today, much of the recorded music used in commercial radio stations is on magnetic tape or compact disc. Disc jockeys are still very much a part of the radio station's image, with major players commanding top salaries.

THE JOB

Disc jockeys serve as a bridge between music and listener. They also perform such public services as announcing the time, the weather forecast, or important news. Working at a radio station can be a lonely job, since often the DJ is the only person in the studio. But because their job is to maintain the good spirits of their audience and attract new listeners, disc jockeys must possess the ability to sound relaxed and cheerful.

Dave Wineland is a disc jockey at WRZQ 107.3 in Columbus, Indiana. He once worked the popular 5:30–10:00 A.M. morning shift that many commuters listen to on their way to work, but now works the afternoon shift. Like many DJs, his duties extend beyond on-air announcements. He also works as production director at the station and writes and produces many of the commercials and promotion announcements. "I spend a lot of time in the production room," says Wineland, who also delegates some of the production duties to other DJs on the staff.

Unlike the more conventional radio or television announcer, the disc jockey does not follow a written script. Except for the commercial announcements, which must be read as they are written, the DJ's statements are usually spontaneous. DJs are not usually required to play a musical selection to the end; they may fade out a record when it interferes with a predetermined schedule for commercials, news, time checks, or weather reports. DJs are not always free to play what they want; at some radio stations, especially the larger ones, the program director or the music director makes the decisions about the music that will be played. And while some stations may encourage their disc jockeys to talk, others emphasize music over commentary and restrict the amount of ad-libbing, or spontaneous talking, that DJs can do.

Many DJs have become well-known public personalities in broadcasting; they may participate in community activities and public events.

Disc jockeys who work at parties and other special events usually work on a part-time basis. They are often called *party DJs*. A DJ who works for a supplying company receives training, equipment, music, and job assignments from the company. Self-employed DJs must provide everything they need themselves. Party DJs have more contact with people than radio DJs, so they must be personable with clients.

REQUIREMENTS

High School

You can start to prepare for a career as a disc jockey during high school. A good knowledge of the English language, correct pronunciation, and diction are important. High school English and speech classes are helpful in getting a good familiarity with the language. Extracurricular activities such as debating and theater will also help you learn good pronunciation and projection. Music classes will introduce you to musical styles, techniques, and artists.

Many high schools have radio stations on site where students can work as DJs, production managers, or technicians. This experience can be a good starting point to learn more about the field. Dave Wineland's first radio job was at the radio station at Carmel High School in Indianapolis.

Postsecondary Training

Although there are no formal educational requirements for becoming a disc jockey, many large stations prefer applicants with a college education. Some students choose to attend a school specifically for broadcasting, taking courses specific to becoming an announcer. However, students should research the school's reputation by getting references from the school or the local Better Business Bureau. Many other hopeful DJs obtain a more general degree in communications. Like many disc jockeys today, Wineland has a college degree. He earned a degree in telecommunications from Ball State University.

Although prospective employers may not have specific training requirements, station officials pay particular attention to applicants' taped auditions. Companies that hire DJs for parties will often train them; experience is not always necessary if the applicant has a suitable personality.

Other Requirements

Disc jockeys should be levelheaded and able to react calmly even in the face of a crisis. Many unexpected circumstances can arise that demand the skill of quick thinking. For example, if guests who are to appear on a program either do not arrive or become too nervous to go on the air, the DJ must fill the airtime. He or she must also smooth over a breakdown in equipment or some other technical difficulty.

Union membership may be required for employment with large stations in major cities. The largest talent union is the American Federation of Television and Radio Artists. Most small stations, however, hire nonunion workers.

EXPLORING

Reading publications will help you learn more about the radio industry. *Radio & Records* (in print and online at http://www.rronline.com) is one of the most popular publications for those involved in the radio business. It contains news on radio happenings, formats, a directory of organizations and services related to the field, and job listings.

If a career as a DJ sounds interesting, you might try to get a summer job at a radio station. Although you may not get a chance to work on air, working behind the scenes will allow you to gauge whether or not that kind of work appeals to you.

Take advantage of any opportunity you get to speak or perform before an audience. Appearing as a speaker or a performer can help you decide whether or not you have the necessary stage presence for a career on the air.

Many colleges and universities have their own radio stations and offer courses in radio. Students can gain valuable experience working at college-owned stations. Some radio stations offer students financial assistance and on-the-job training in the form of internships and co-op work programs, as well as scholarships and fellowships.

EMPLOYERS

There has been a steady growth in the number of radio stations in the United States. According to 2002 statistics from the National Association of Broadcasters, the United States alone has 13,296 radio stations.

Radio is a 24-hour-a-day, seven-day-a-week medium, so there are many slots to fill. Most of these stations are small stations where disc jockeys are required to perform many other duties for a lower salary than at larger stations in bigger metropolitan areas.

Since the passage of the Telecommunications Act of 1996, companies can own an unlimited number of radio stations nationwide with an eight-station limit within one market area, depending on the size of the market. When this legislation took effect, mergers and acquisitions changed the face of the radio industry. So, while the pool of employers is smaller, the number of stations continues to rise.

STARTING OUT

One way to enter this field is to apply for an entry-level job rather than a job as a disc jockey. It is also advisable to start at a small local station. As opportunities arise, DJs commonly move from one station to another.

While still a high school student, Dave Wineland applied for a position at his local radio station in Monticello, Indiana. "I was willing to work long hours for low pay," he says, acknowledging that starting out in radio can require some sacrifices. However, on-air experience is a must.

An announcer is employed only after an audition. Audition material should be selected carefully to show the prospective employer the range of the applicant's abilities. A prospective DJ should practice talking aloud, alone, then make a tape of him- or herself with five to seven minutes of material to send to radio stations. The tape should include a news story, two 60-second commercials, and a sample of the applicant introducing and coming out of a record. (Tapes should not include the whole song, just the first and final few seconds, with the aspiring DJ introducing and finishing the music; this is called *telescoping.*) In addition to presenting prepared materials, applicants may also be asked to read material that they have not seen previously. This may be a commercial, news release, dramatic selection, or poem.

ADVANCEMENT

Most successful disc jockeys advance from small stations to large ones. The typical experienced DJ will have held several jobs at different types of stations.

Some careers lead from being a DJ to other types of radio or television work. More people are employed in sales, promotion, and planning than in performing, and they are often paid more than DJs.

EARNINGS

The salary range for disc jockeys is extremely broad, with a low of $12,770 in 2002, according to the U.S. Department of Labor (USDL), and a high of more than $1 million for popular broadcast personalities such as Howard Stern. The average salary in 2002 was $20,620, according to the USDL.

Smaller market areas and smaller stations fall closer to the bottom of the range, while the top markets and top-rated stations offer DJs higher salaries.

Benefits vary according to the size of the market and station. However, vacation and sick time is somewhat limited because the medium requires that radio personalities be on the air nearly every day.

WORK ENVIRONMENT

Work in radio stations is usually very pleasant. Almost all stations are housed in modern facilities. Temperature and dust control are important factors in the proper maintenance of technical electronic equipment, and people who work around such machinery benefit from the precautions taken to preserve it.

The work can be demanding. It requires that every activity or comment on the air begins and ends exactly on time. This can be difficult, especially when the disc jockey has to handle news, commercials, music, weather, and guests within a certain time frame. It takes a lot of skill to work the controls, watch the clock, select music, talk with a caller or guest, read reports, and entertain the audience; a DJ must often perform several of these tasks simultaneously. A DJ must be able to plan ahead and stay alert so that when one song ends he or she is ready with the next song or with a scheduled commercial.

Because radio audiences listen to DJs who play the music they like and talk about the things that interest them, DJs must always be aware of pleasing their audience. If listeners begin switching stations, ratings go down and disc jockeys can lose their jobs.

Disc jockeys do not always have job security; if the owner or manager of a radio station changes, the DJ may lose his or her job. The consolidation of radio stations to form larger, cost-efficient stations has caused some employees to lose their jobs.

DJs may work irregular hours. They may have to report for work at a very early hour in the morning. Sometimes they will be free during the daytime hours, but will have to work late into the night. Many radio stations operate on a 24-hour basis. All-night announcers may be alone in the station during their working hours.

The disc jockey who stays with a station for a period of time becomes a well-known personality in the community. Such celebrities are sought after as participants in community activities and may be recognized on the street.

DJs who work at parties and other events find themselves in a variety of settings. They generally have more freedom to choose music selections but little opportunity to ad-lib. They work primarily on evenings and weekends.

OUTLOOK

According to the National Association of Broadcasters, radio reaches 78 percent of all consumers every day. Despite radio's popularity, the *Occupational Outlook Handbook* projects that employment of announcers will decline slightly over the next several years. Due to this decline, competition for jobs will be great in an already competitive field.

While small stations will still hire beginners, on-air experience will become increasingly important. Another area where job seekers can push ahead of the competition is in specialization. Knowledge of specific areas such as business, consumer, and health news may work to an applicant's advantage.

While on-air radio personalities are not necessarily affected by economic downturns, mergers and changes in the industry can affect employment. If a radio station has to make cuts due to a weak economy, it will most likely do so in a behind-the-scenes area, which means that the disc jockeys who remain may face a further diversity in their duties.

Fewer positions may also be available to disc jockeys in the future due to voice-tracking, which is when a DJ prerecords a radio show for one or more shifts in one or more cities. Voice-tracking saves radio companies money by allowing the work of one DJ to be used in a variety of settings and time slots. Of course, voice-tracking cannot be used for talk shows, remote broadcasts, or live concerts. The industry is divided on how this new trend will affect the radio industry as a whole.

FOR MORE INFORMATION

Visit the BEA website for useful information about broadcast education and the broadcasting industry.
Broadcast Education Association
1771 N Street, NW
Washington, DC 20036
Tel: 888-380-7222
http://www.beaweb.org

For broadcast education, support, and scholarship information, contact
National Association of Broadcasters
1771 N Street, NW
Washington, DC 20036
Tel: 202-429-5300
http://www.nab.org

For scholarship and internship information, contact
Radio-Television News Directors Association & Foundation
1600 K Street, NW, Suite 700
Washington, DC 20006
Tel: 202-659-6510
http://www.rtnda.org

For career information and an overview of the industry, visit
About.com: Radio
http://radio.about.com

Music Agents and Scouts

OVERVIEW

An agent is a salesperson who sells artistic talent. *Music agents* act as the representatives for musical performers such as musicians, singers, orchestras, bands, and other musical groups, promoting their talent and managing legal contractual business. *Music scouts* search for musical talent at clubs, concert halls, and other music venues.

HISTORY

As the music industry developed into a powerful force in the United States in the last half of the 20th century, resourceful business-minded people became agents when they realized that there was money to be made by controlling access to musical talent. They became middlemen between musical artists and the recording industry and owners of musical venues, charging commissions for use of their clients.

Currently, commissions range between 10 and 20 percent of the money a musical act earns for a performance. In more recent years, agents have negotiated revolutionary deals for their musical stars, making more money for agencies and musicians alike. In addition, today's music agents handle most, if not all, aspects of a musician's career, from commercial endorsements to financial investments.

THE JOB

Music agents act as representatives for all types of musicians. They look for clients who have potential for success and then work aggressively to promote their clients to owners of concert halls, clubs, theaters, musical festivals, and other venues where musicians perform. Agents work closely with clients to find assignments that will best achieve their clients' career goals. Some music agents specialize in one musical genre such as rap, classical, or rock.

Music agents find clients in several ways. Those employed by an agency might be assigned a client by the agency, based on experience or a compatible personality. Some music agents also work as *talent scouts* and actively search for new clients, whom they then bring to an agency, or the clients themselves might approach agents who have good reputations and request their representation. Music agents listen to recordings of the band or singer's music, visit clubs and other music venues to observe talent firsthand, attend musical showcases, and conduct live auditions to determine what musical acts they would like to represent. All agents consider a client's potential for a long career—it is important to find performers who will grow, develop their skills, and eventually create a continuing demand for their talents.

When an agent agrees to represent a client, they both sign a contract that specifies the extent of representation, the time period, payment, and other legal considerations.

When agents look for jobs for their clients, they do not necessarily try to find as many assignments as possible. Agents try to carefully choose assignments that will further their clients' careers. For example, an agent might represent a musician who wants to graduate from smaller musical clubs to large outdoor venues such as stadiums. The agent looks for opportunities to place their artists in these settings, perhaps by having them perform as an opening act for a stadium tour for a major headliner such as the Rolling Stones, Britney Spears, or Shania Twain. If their artists are positively received by the audience and concert promoter, they may be asked to headline a stadium tour at a later date.

Agents also work closely with the potential employers of their clients. They keep in touch with music venue owners, recording industry executives, and other industry professionals to see if any of their clients can meet their needs.

When agents see a possible match between employer and client, they speak to both and quickly organize meetings, interviews, or auditions so that employers can meet potential hires and evaluate their musical ability. Agents must be persistent and aggressive on behalf of their clients. They spend time on the phone with employers, convincing them of their clients' talents and persuading them to hire clients. There may be one or several interviews, and the agent may coach clients through this process to make sure clients understand what the employer is looking for and adapt their performances accordingly. When a client achieves success and is in great demand, the agent receives calls and other types of work requests and passes along only those that are appropriate to the interests and goals of his or her client.

When an employer agrees to hire a client, the agent helps negotiate a contract that outlines salary, benefits, promotional appearances, and other fees, rights, and obligations. Agents have to look out for the best interests of their clients and at the same time satisfy employers in order to establish continuing, long-lasting relationships.

Agents often develop lifelong working relationships with their clients. They act as business associates, advisers, advocates, mentors, teachers, guardians, and confidantes. Because of the complicated nature of these relationships, they can also be volatile, so a successful relationship requires trust and respect on both sides; this can only develop through experience and time. Agents who represent high-profile talent comprise only a small percentage of agency work. Most agents represent lesser known or local known talent.

REQUIREMENTS

High School
You should take courses in business, mathematics, and accounting to prepare for the management aspects of an agent's job. Take English and speech courses to develop good communication skills because an agent must be gifted at negotiation. Music classes of all types will help you become familiar with musical styles.

Postsecondary Training
There are no formal requirements for becoming an agent, but a bachelor's degree is strongly recommended. Advanced degrees in law and business are becoming increasingly prevalent; law and business training are useful because agents are responsible for writing contracts according to legal regulations. However, in some cases an agent may obtain this training on the job. Agents come from a variety of backgrounds; some have worked as musicians and then shifted into agent careers because they enjoyed working in the industry. Agents who have law or business degrees have an advantage when it comes to advancing their careers or opening a new agency.

Certification or Licensing
Many states require music agents to be licensed. Contact officials in the state in which you are interested in working for specific requirements.

Other Requirements

Music agents need to be willing to work hard and aggressively pursue opportunities for clients. You should be detail-oriented and have a good head for business; contract work requires meticulous attention to detail. You need a great deal of self-motivation and ambition to develop good contacts. You should be comfortable talking with all kinds of people and be able to develop relationships easily. It helps to be a good general conversationalist in addition to being knowledgeable about music.

EXPLORING

Learn as much as you can about the music industry. Read publications agents read, such as *Billboard* (http://www.billboard.com), *Variety* (http://www.variety.com), or *Radio & Records* (http://www.rronline.com). Listen to current musical acts to get a sense of the established and up-and-coming talents in the music industry.

If you live in Los Angeles, New York, or Nashville, you may be able to volunteer or intern at an agency to find out more about the career. If you live outside these cities, check the Yellow Pages or search the Web for listings of local agencies. Most major cities have agents who represent local musicians. If you contact them, they may be willing to offer you some insight into the nature of talent management in general.

EMPLOYERS

The largest music agencies are located in Los Angeles, New York City, and Nashville, where the music industry is centered. There are music agencies in most large cities, however, and independent agents are established throughout the country.

STARTING OUT

The best way to enter this field is to seek an internship with an agency. If you live in or can spend a summer in Los Angeles, New York, or Nashville, you have an advantage in terms of numbers of opportunities. Libraries and bookstores will have resources for locating talent agencies. By searching the Web, you can find many free listings of reputable agents. The Yellow Pages will yield a list of local talent agencies. Compile a list of agencies that offer internship opportunities. Some internships will be paid and others may provide college course credit, but most importantly, they will provide you with experience and contacts in the industry. An intern who works hard and knows something about the music business stands a good chance of securing an entry-level position at an agency. At the top agencies, this will be a position in the mail room, where almost everyone starts. In smaller agencies, it may be an assistant position. Eventually persistence, hard work, and good connections will lead to a job as an agent.

ADVANCEMENT

Once you have a job as an assistant, you will be allowed to work closely with a music agent to learn the ropes. You may be able to read contracts and listen in on phone calls and meetings. You will begin to take on some of your own clients as you gain experience. Agents who wish to advance must work aggressively on behalf of their clients as well as seek out quality talent to bring into an agency. Successful agents command more lucrative salaries and may choose to open their own agencies. Some agents find that their work is a good stepping stone toward a different career in the music industry, such as a talent buyer for a music club or an artist and repertoire worker in the recording industry.

EARNINGS

Earnings for agents vary greatly, depending on the success of the agent and his or her clients. An agency receives 10 to 20 percent of a client's fee for a project. An agent is then paid a commission by the agency as well as a base salary. The U.S. Department of Labor reports that agents and business managers of artists, performers, and athletes earned median salaries of $55,730 in 2002. The lowest paid 10 percent earned less than $24,910, and the highest paid 10 percent $130,290 or more annually. However, music agents employed by top agencies earn much higher salaries.

Experienced agents employed by agencies will receive health and retirement benefits, bonuses, and paid travel and accommodations. Agents who are self-employed must provide their own heath insurance and other benefits.

WORK ENVIRONMENT

Work in a talent agency can be lively and exciting. Music agents find it rewarding to watch a client attain success with their help. This work can seem very glamorous, allowing music agents to rub elbows with the rich and famous and make contacts with the most powerful people in the music industry. Most agents, however, represent less-famous musicians.

Agents' work requires a great deal of stamina and determination in the face of setbacks. The work can be extremely stressful, even in small agencies. It often demands long hours, including evenings and weekends. To stay successful, agents at the top of the industry must constantly network. They spend a great deal of time on the telephone, with both clients and others in the industry, and attending industry functions.

OUTLOOK

Employment in the music and entertainment field is expected to grow rapidly in response to the demand for entertainment from a growing population. However, the number of musicians also continues to grow, creating fierce competition for all jobs in this industry. This competition will drive the need for more music agents and scouts to find talented individuals and place them in the best jobs. This is a very difficult career to break into, and most successful music agents spend years building their experience and client list in smaller markets before they enjoy a modicum of success.

FOR MORE INFORMATION

The following are some of the largest music talent agencies in the world:

International Creative Management
8942 Wilshire Boulevard
Beverly Hills, CA 90211
http://www.icmtalent.com/musperf/musperf.html

William Morris Agency
One William Morris Place
Beverly Hills, CA 90212
http://www.wma.com

The following organization represents performing arts agents and managers:

North American Performing Arts Managers and Agents
459 Columbus Avenue, #133
New York, NY 10024
http://www.napama.org

Musical Instrument Repairers and Tuners

OVERVIEW

Musical instrument repairers and tuners work on a variety of instruments, often operating inside music shops or repair shops to keep the pieces in tune and in proper condition. Those who specialize in working on pianos or pipe organs may travel to the instrument's location to work. Instrument repairers and tuners usually specialize in certain families of musical instruments, such as stringed or brass instruments. Depending on the instrument, they may be skilled in working with wood, metal, electronics, or other materials. There are approximately 8,000 music instrument repairers and tuners employed in the United States.

HISTORY

The world's first musical instrument was the human body. Paleolithic dancers clapped, stamped, chanted, and slapped their bodies to mark rhythm. Gourd rattles, bone whistles, scrapers, hollow branch, and conch shell trumpets, wooden rhythm pounders and knockers, and bullroarers followed. By the early Neolithic times, people had developed drums that produced two or more pitches and pottery and cane flutes that gave several notes. The musical bow, a primitive stringed instrument and forerunner of the jaw harp, preceded the bow-shaped harp (about 3000 B.C.) and the long-necked lute (about 2000 B.C.).

QUICK FACTS

School Subjects
Music
Technical/shop

Personal Skills
Artistic
Mechanical/manipulative

Work Environment
Primarily indoors
One location with some travel

Minimum Education Level
Some postsecondary training

Salary Range
$16,160 to $29,440 to $61,400+

Certification or Licensing
Voluntary

Outlook
More slowly than the average

DOT
730

GOE
05.05.12

NOC
7445

O*NET-SOC
49-9063.00, 49-9063.01, 49-9063.02, 49-9063.03, 49-9063.04

Students in the band instrument repair program at Minnesota State College-Southeast Technical repair musical instruments in a lab. (*John Huth, Minnesota State College-Southeast Technical*)

The history of the pipe organ stretches back to the third century B.C., when the Egyptians developed an organ that used water power to produce a stream of air. A few centuries later, organs appeared in Byzantium that used bellows (a device that draws air in and then expels it with great force) to send air through the organ pipes. From that time until about A.D. 1500 all the features of the modern pipe organ were developed.

The first version of the violin, played by scraping a taut bow across several stretched strings, appeared in Europe around 1510. The end of the 16th century saw the development of the violin as it is known today. Over the next hundred years, violin making reached its greatest achievements in the area around Cremona, Italy, where families of master craftsmen, such as the Stradivaris, the Guarneris, and the Amatis, set a standard for quality that never has been surpassed. Today, their violins are coveted by players around the world for their tonal quality.

The modern piano is the end product of a gradual evolution from plucked string instruments, such as the harp, to instruments employing hammers of one kind or another to produce notes by striking the strings. By the late 1700s, the immediate ancestor of the modern piano had been developed. Improvements and modifications (most involving new materials or manufacturing processes) took place throughout the 19th century, resulting in today's piano.

In addition to the stringed instruments, contemporary orchestral instruments also include the woodwind, brass, and percussion families. Woodwinds include the flute, clarinet, oboe, bassoon, and saxophone. Brass instruments include the French horn, trumpet, cornet, trombone, and tuba. All require some professional care and maintenance at some time. The modern electronic organ is a descendent of the pipe organ. In 1934, Laurens Hammond, an American inventor, patented the first practical electronic organ, an instrument that imitates the sound of the pipe organ but requires much less space and is more economical and practical to own and operate. The development of electronic and computer technology produced the first synthesizers and synthesized instruments, which are used widely today.

THE JOB

All but the most heavily damaged instruments usually can be repaired by competent, experienced craftsworkers. In addition, instruments require regular maintenance and inspection to ensure that they play properly and to prevent small problems from becoming major ones.

Stringed-instrument repairers perform extremely detailed and difficult work. The repair of violins, violas, and cellos might be considered the finest woodworking done in the world today. Because their sound quality is so beautiful, some older, rarer violins are worth millions of dollars, and musicians will sometimes fly halfway around the world to have rare instruments repaired by master restorers. In many ways, the work of these master craftspeople may be compared to the restoration of fine art masterpieces.

When a violin or other valuable stringed instrument needs repair, its owner takes the instrument to a repair shop, which may employ many repairers. If the violin has cracks in its body, it must be taken apart. The pieces of a violin are held together by a special glue that allows the instrument to be dismantled easily for repair purposes. The glue, which is made from hides and bones and has been used for more than 400 years, is sturdy but does not bond permanently with the wood.

To repair a crack in the back of a violin, the repairer first pops the back off the instrument. After cleaning the crack with warm water, the repairer glues the crack and attaches cleats or studs above the crack on the inside to prevent further splitting. The repairer reassembles the violin and closes the outside of the crack with fill varnish.

Lastly, the repairer treats the crack scrupulously with retouch varnish so that it becomes invisible.

The repairer does not complete every step immediately after the previous one. Depending on the age and value of the instrument, a repair job can take three weeks or longer. Glues and varnishes need to set, and highly detailed work demands much concentration. The repairer also needs to do research to isolate the original type of varnish on the instrument and match it precisely with modern materials. The repairer usually has more than one repair job going at any one time.

A major restoration, such as the replacement of old patchwork or the fitting of inside patches to support the instrument, requires even more time. A large project can take two years or longer. A master restorer can put 2,000 or more hours into the repair of a valuable violin that has nothing more than a few cracks in its finish. Since many fine instruments are worth $2 million or more, they need intense work to preserve the superior quality of their sound. The repairer cannot rush the work, must concentrate on every detail, and complete the repair properly or risk other problems later on.

While all instruments are not made by Stradivari, they still need to be kept in good condition to be played well. Owners bring in their violins, violas, and cellos to the repair shop every season for cleaning, inspecting joints, and gluing gaps. The work involves tools similar to woodworker's tools, such as carving knives, planes, and gouges. The violin repairer will often need to play the instrument to check its condition and tune it. *Bow rehairers* maintain the quality of the taut, vibrating horsehair string that is stretched from end to end of the resilient wooden bow.

Wind-instrument repairers require a similar level of skill to that required of stringed-instrument repairers. However, as the quality of sound is more standard among manufacturers, old instruments do not necessarily play any better than new ones, and these instruments do not command the same value as a fine violin.

The repairer first needs to determine the extent of repairs that the instrument warrants. The process may range from a few minor repairs to bring the instrument up to playing condition to a complete overhaul. After fixing the instrument, the repairer also will clean both the inside and outside and may replate the metal finish on a scuffed or rusty instrument.

For woodwinds such as clarinets and oboes, common repairs include fixing or replacing the moving parts of the instrument, including replacing broken keys with new keys, cutting new padding or corks to replace worn pieces, and replacing springs. If the body of the woodwind is cracked in any sections the repairer will take the instrument apart and attempt to pin or glue the crack shut. In some situations, the repairer will replace the entire section or joint of the instrument.

Repairing brass instruments such as trumpets and French horns requires skill in metal working and plating. The pieces of these instruments are held together by solder, which the repairer must heat and remove to take the instrument apart for repair work. To fix dents, the repairer will unsolder the piece and work the dent out with hammers and more delicate tools and seal splits in the metal with solder as well. A final buffing and polishing usually removes any evidence of the repair.

If one of the valves of the brass instrument is leaking, the repairer may replate it and build up layers of metal to fill the gaps. At times, the repairer will replace a badly damaged valve with a new valve from the instrument manufacturer, but often the owner will discard the entire instrument because the cost of making a new valve from raw materials is prohibitive. Replacement parts are usually available from the manufacturer, but parts for older instruments are sometimes difficult or impossible to find. For this reason, many repairers save and stockpile discarded instruments for their parts.

Piano technicians and *piano tuners* repair and tune pianos so that when a key is struck it will produce its correctly pitched note of the musical scale. A piano may go out of tune for a variety of reasons, including strings that have stretched or tightened from age, temperature change, relocation, or through use. Tuners use a special wrench to adjust the pins that control the tension on the strings. Piano tuners usually are specially trained for such work, but piano technicians also may perform tuning in connection with a more thorough inspection or overhaul of an instrument.

A piano's performance is also affected by problems in any of the thousands of moving parts of the action or by problems in the sounding board or the frame holding the strings. These are problems that the technician is trained to analyze and correct. They may involve replacing or repairing parts or making adjustments that enable the existing parts to function more smoothly.

The life of a piano—that is, the period of time before it can no longer be properly tuned or adjusted to correct operational problems—is usually estimated at 20 years. Because the harp and strong outer wooden frame are seldom damaged, technicians often rebuild pianos by replacing the sounding board and strings, refurbishing and replacing parts where necessary, and refinishing the outer case.

In all their work, from tuning to rebuilding, piano technicians discover a piano's problems by talking to the owner and playing the instrument themselves. They may dismantle a piano partially on-site to determine the amount of wear to its parts and look for broken parts. They use common hand tools such as hammers, screwdrivers, and pliers. To repair and rebuild pianos, they use a variety of specialized tools for stringing and setting pins.

For *pipe organ technicians,* the largest part of the job is repairing and maintaining existing organs. This primarily involves tuning the pipes, which can be time consuming, even in a moderate-sized organ.

To tune a flue pipe, the technician moves a slide that increases or decreases the length of the speaking (note-producing) part of the pipe, varying its pitch. The technician tunes a reed pipe varying the length of the brass reed inside the pipe.

To tune an organ, the technician tunes either the A or C pipes by matching their notes with those of a tuning fork or electronic note-producing device. He or she then tunes the other pipes in harmony with the A or C notes. This may require a day or more for a moderate-sized organ and much longer for a giant concert organ.

Pipe organ technicians also diagnose, locate, and correct problems in the operating parts of the organ and perform preventive maintenance on a regular basis. To do this, they work with electric wind-generating equipment and with slides, valves, keys, air channels, and other equipment that enables the organist to produce the desired music.

Occasionally, a new organ is installed in a new or existing structure. Manufacturers design and install the largest organs. Each is unique, and the designer carefully supervises its construction and installation. Often, designers individually create moderate-sized organs specifically for the structure, usually churches, in which they will be played. Technicians follow the designer's blueprints closely during installation. The work involves assembling and connecting premanufactured components, using a variety of hand and power tools. Technicians may work in teams, especially when installing the largest pipes of the organ.

Although the electronic organ imitates the sound of the pipe organ, the workings of the two instruments have little in common. The electronic organ consists of electrical and electronic components and circuits that channel electrical current through various oscillators and amplifiers to produce sound when a player presses each key. It is rare for an oscillator or other component to need adjustment in the way an organ pipe needs to be adjusted to tune it. A technician tunes an electronic organ by testing it for electronic malfunction and replacing or repairing the component, circuit board, or wire.

The work of the *electronic organ technician* is closer to that of the television repair technician than it is to that of the pipe organ technician. The technician often begins looking for the source of a problem by checking for loose wires and solder connections. After making routine checks, technicians consult wiring diagrams that enable them to trace and test the circuits of the entire instrument to find malfunctions. For instance, an unusual or irregular voltage in a circuit may indicate a problem. Once the problem has been located, the technician often solves it by replacing a malfunctioning part, such as a circuit board.

These technicians work with common electrician's tools: pliers, wire cutters, screwdriver, soldering iron, and testing equipment. Technicians can make most repairs and adjustments in the customer's home. Because each manufacturer's instruments are arranged differently, technicians follow manufacturers' wiring diagrams and service manuals to locate trouble spots and make repairs. In larger and more complex instruments, such as those in churches and theaters, this may require a day or more of searching and testing.

Other types of repairers work on a variety of less common instruments. *Percussion tuners and repairers* work on drums, bells, congas, timbales, cymbals, and castanets. They may stretch new skins over the instrument, replace broken or missing parts, or seal cracks in the wood.

Accordion tuners and repairers work on free-reed portable accordions, piano accordions, concertinas, harmoniums, and harmonicas. They repair leaks in the bellows of an instrument, replace broken or damaged reeds, and perform various maintenance tasks. Other specialists in instrument repair include fretted-instrument repairers, harp regulators, trombone-slide assemblers, metal-reed tuners, tone regulators, and chip tuners.

Some musical repairers work as *musical instrument designers and builders*. They work in musical instrument factories or as freelancers designing and building instruments in their own workshops. Almost any type of instrument can be designed and built, but musical instrument builders most often craft guitars, banjos, violins, and flutes.

In addition to repairing, designing, or building instruments, those who run their own shops perform duties similar to others in the retail business. They order stock from instrument manufacturers, wait on customers, handle their accounting and billing work, and perform other duties.

REQUIREMENTS
High School
No matter what family of instruments interests you, you should start preparing for this field by gaining a basic knowledge of music. Take

high school classes in music history, music theory, and choir, chorus, or other singing classes. By learning to read music, developing an ear for scales, and understanding tones and pitches, you will be developing an excellent background for this work. Also, explore your interest in instruments (besides your own voice) by taking band or orchestra classes or private music lessons. By learning how to play an instrument, you will also learn how a properly tuned and maintained instrument should sound. If you find yourself interested in instruments with metal parts, consider taking art or shop classes that provide the opportunity to do metal working. These classes will allow you to practice soldering and work with appropriate tools. If you are interested in piano or stringed instruments, consider taking art or shop classes that offer woodworking. In these classes you will learn finishing techniques and use tools that you may relate to the building and maintaining of the bodies of these instruments.

Because instrument repair of any type is precision work, you will benefit from taking mathematics classes such as algebra and geometry. Since many instrument repairers and tuners are self-employed, take business or accounting classes to prepare for this possibility. Finally, take English classes to develop your research, reading, and communication skills. You will often need to consult technical instruction manuals for repair and maintenance work. You will also need strong communication skills that will help you broaden your client base as well as help you explain to your clients what work needs to be done.

Postsecondary Training

There are two main routes to becoming a music instrument repairer and tuner: extensive apprenticeship or formal education through technical or vocational schools. Apprenticeships, however, can be difficult to find. You will simply need to contact instrument repair shops and request a position as a trainee. Once you have found a position, the training period may last from two to five years. You will get hands-on experience working with the instruments as well as having other duties around the shop, such as selling any products offered.

Depending on the family of instruments you want to work with, there are a number of technical or vocational schools that offer either courses or full-time programs in repair and maintenance work. Professional organizations may have information on such schools. The National Association of Professional Band Instrument Repair Technicians, for example, provides a listing of schools offering programs in band instrument repair. The Piano Technicians Guild has information on both full-time programs and correspondence courses.

Wind-instrument repairers can learn their craft at one of the handful of vocational schools in the country that offers classes in instrument repair. Entrance requirements vary among schools, but all require at least a high school diploma or GED. Typical classes that are part of any type of instrument repair and tuning education include acoustics, tool care and operation, and small business practices. Depending on what instrument you choose to specialize in, you may also study topics such as buffing, dent removal, plating, soldering, or woodworking. You may also be required to invest in personal hand tools and supplies, and you may need to make tools that are not available from suppliers.

If you are interested in working with electronic organs, you will need at least one year of electronics technical training to learn organ repair skills. Electronics training is available from community colleges and technical and vocational schools. The U.S. Armed Forces also offer excellent training in electronics, which you can apply to instrument work. Electronic organ technicians also may attend training courses offered by electronic organ manufacturers.

It is important to keep in mind that even those who take courses or attend school for their postsecondary training will need to spend years honing their skills.

A number of instrument repairers and tuners have completed some college work or have a bachelor's degree. A 1997 Piano Technicians Guild survey (the most recent available), for example, showed that at least 50 percent of their members had bachelor's degrees or higher. Although no colleges award bachelor's degrees in instrument repair, people who major in some type of music performance may find this background adds to their understanding of the work.

Certification or Licensing
The Piano Technicians Guild helps its members improve their skills and keep up with developments in piano technology. Refresher courses and seminars in new developments are offered by local chapters, and courses offered by manufacturers are publicized in Guild publications. The Guild also administers a series of tests that can lead to certification as a registered piano technician.

Other Requirements
Personal qualifications for people in this occupational group include keen hearing and eyesight, mechanical aptitude, and manual dexterity. You should be resourceful and able to learn on the job, because every instrument that needs repair is unique and requires individual care. You must also have the desire to learn throughout your profes-

sional life by studying trade magazines and manufacturers' service manuals related to new developments in their field. You can also improve your skills in training programs and at regional and national seminars. Instrument manufacturers often offer training in the repair of their particular products.

Other qualifications for this career relate to your instrument specialty. For example, if you want to work as a piano technician, you should be able to communicate clearly when talking about a piano's problems and when advising a customer. A pleasant manner and good appearance are important to instill confidence. While the physical strength required for moving a piano is not often needed, you may be required to bend or stand in awkward positions while working on the piano. If you are interested in working as a pipe organ technician, you will need the ability to follow blueprints and printed instructions to plan and execute repair or installation work. And any repairer and tuner who works in a store selling musical instruments should be comfortable working with the public.

EXPLORING

One of the best ways to explore this field is to take some type of musical instrument lessons. This experience will help you develop an ear for tonal quality and acquaint you with the care of your instrument. It will also put you in contact with those who work professionally with music. You may develop a contact with someone at the store where you have purchased or rented your instrument, and, naturally, you will get to know your music teacher. Ask these people what they know about the repair and tuning business. Your high school or local college music departments can also be excellent places for meeting those who work with instruments. Ask teachers in these departments whom they know working in instrument repair. You may be able to set up an informational interview with a repairer and tuner you find through these contacts. Ask the repairer about his or her education, how he or she got interested in the work, what he or she would recommend for someone considering the field, and any other questions you may have.

Part-time and summer jobs that are related closely to this occupation may be difficult to obtain because full-time trainees usually handle the routine tasks of a helper. Nevertheless, it is worth applying for such work at music stores and repair shops in case they do not use full-time trainees. General clerical jobs in stores that sell musical instruments may help familiarize you with the language of the field and may offer you the opportunity to observe skilled repairers at work.

EMPLOYERS

Approximately 8,000 people work as musical instrument repairers and tuners of all types in the United States. About one-fourth of this number are self-employed and may operate out of their own homes. The majority of the rest work in repair shops and music stores and for manufacturers. Large cities with extensive professional music activity, both in the United States and in Europe, are the best places for employment. Musical centers such as Chicago, New York, London, and Vienna are the hubs of the repair business for stringed instruments, and any repairer who wishes a sufficient amount of work may have to relocate to one of these cities.

Some piano technicians work in factories where pianos are made. They may assemble and adjust pianos or inspect the finished instruments. Some technicians work in shops that rebuild pianos. Many piano repairers and tuners work in customers' homes.

Most of the few hundred pipe organ technicians in the United States are self-employed. These pipe organ technicians are primarily engaged in repairing and tuning existing organs. A small number are employed by organ manufacturers and are engaged in testing and installing new instruments. The great expense involved in manufacturing and installing a completely new pipe organ decreases demand and makes this type of work scarce.

STARTING OUT

Vocational schools and community colleges that offer instrument repair training can usually connect recent graduates with repair shops that have job openings. Those who enter the field through apprenticeships work at the local shop where they are receiving their training. Professional organizations may also have information on job openings.

ADVANCEMENT

Repairers and tuners may advance their skills by participating in special training programs. A few who work for large dealers or repair shops may move into supervisory positions. Some instrument repair technicians become instructors in music instrument repair programs at community colleges and technical institutes.

Another path to advancement is to open one's own musical repair shop and service. Before doing this, however, the worker should have adequate training to survive the strong competition that exists in the tuning and repair business. In many cases, repairers may need to continue working for another employer until they develop a clientele large enough to support a full-time business.

A few restorers of stringed instruments earn worldwide reputations for their exceptional skill. Their earnings and the caliber of their customers both rise significantly when they become well known. It takes a great deal of hard work and talent to achieve such professional standing, however, and this recognition only comes after years in the field. At any one time, there may be perhaps 10 restorers in the world who perform exceptional work, while another 100 or so are known for doing very good work. The work of these few craftspeople is always in great demand.

EARNINGS

Wages vary depending on geographic area and the worker's specialty, skill, and speed at making repairs. Full-time instrument repairers and tuners had a median income of $29,440 in 2002, according to the U.S. Department of Labor. The highest paid 10 percent earned $61,400 or more per year, and the lowest paid earned less than $16,160 annually. Some helpers work for the training they get and receive no pay. Repairers and tuners who are self-employed earn more than those who work for music stores or instrument manufacturers, but their income is generally less stable. Repairers who gain an international reputation for the quality of their work earn the highest income in this field.

Repairers and tuners working as employees of manufacturers or stores often receive some benefits, including health insurance, vacation days, and holiday and sick pay. Self-employed repairers and tuners must provide these for themselves.

WORK ENVIRONMENT

Repairers and tuners work in shops, homes, and instrument factories, surrounded by the tools and materials of their trade. The atmosphere is somewhat quiet but the pace is often busy. Since repairers and tuners are usually paid by the piece, they have to concentrate and work diligently on their repairs. Piano technicians and tuners generally perform their work in homes, schools, churches, and other places where pianos are located.

Instrument tuners and repairers may work more than 40 hours a week, especially during the fall and winter, when people spend more time indoors playing musical instruments. Self-employed tuners and repairers often work evenings and weekends, when it is more convenient to meet with customers.

As noted, many repairs demand extreme care and often long periods of time to complete. For large instruments, such as pianos and pipe organs, repairers and tuners may have to work in cramped locations for some length of time, bending, stretching, and using tools that require physical strength to handle. Tuning pianos and organs often requires many hours and can be tedious work.

The field at times may be very competitive, especially among the more prestigious repair shops for stringed instruments. Most people at the major repair shops know each other and vie for the same business. There is often a great deal of pressure from owners to fix their instruments as soon as possible, but a conscientious repairer cannot be rushed into doing a mediocre job. In spite of these drawbacks, repair work is almost always interesting, challenging, and rewarding. Repairers never do the same job twice, and each instrument comes with its own set of challenges. The work requires repairers to call on their ingenuity, skill, and personal pride every day.

OUTLOOK

Job opportunities for musical instrument repairers and tuners are expected to grow more slowly than the average through 2010, according to the U.S. Department of Labor. This is a small, specialized field, and replacement needs will be the source of most jobs. Because training positions and school programs are relatively difficult to find, those with thorough training and education will have the best employment outlook.

It is a luxury for most owners to have their instruments tuned and repaired, and they tend to postpone these services when money is scarce. Tuners and repairers therefore may lose income during economic downturns. In addition, few trainees are hired at repair shops or music stores when business is slow.

FOR MORE INFORMATION

For information on organ and choral music fields, contact
American Guild of Organists
475 Riverside Drive, Suite 1260
New York, NY 10115
Tel: 212-870-2310
http://www.agohq.org

The GAL is an international organization of stringed-instrument makers and repairers. Visit the FAQ section of its website for information on building and repairing instruments and choosing a training program.
Guild of American Luthiers (GAL)
8222 South Park Avenue
Tacoma, WA 98408
Tel: 253-472-7853
http://www.luth.org

For information about band instrument repair and a list of schools offering courses in the field, contact
National Association of Professional Band Instrument Repair
   Technicians, Inc.
PO Box 51
Normal, IL 61761
Tel: 309-452-4257
http://www.napbirt.org

For information on certification, contact
Piano Technicians Guild
4444 Forest Avenue
Kansas City, MO 66106
Tel: 913-432-9975
http://www.ptg.org

––––––––––––––––––––––––––– **INTERVIEW** –––––––––––––––––––––––––––

Minnesota State College-Southeast Technical in Red Wing, Minnesota, is one of only five schools in the United States and Canada that offer training in musical instrument repair. Four faculty members—Ken Cance (woodwinds), Greg Beckwith (brass), David Vincent (guitar), and Lisbeth Nelson Butler (violin family)—teach musical instrument repair at the college. John Huth, a band instrument repair instructor (currently on reassignment at the college), spoke with the editors of Careers in Focus: Music *about the school's program.*

Q. **Please describe the musical instrument repair programs at your school.**

A.   Our school has two programs: band instrument repair (BIR) and musical string instrument repair and building, which has dual study options of violin and guitar. The band instrument repair program has approximately 36 students per year; the violin, 19 students; and the guitar program, 40–50 students.

Our students come from all over the United States. It is rare now that we attract local people—the local employment market has been saturated for years. We get one or two international students a year attending our programs.

Q. What type of musical string instruments do students learn to build?

A. Students can learn how to build acoustic flat top guitars, arch top guitars, mandolins, violins, and electric guitars. These parallel the courses in repair that the students take. Band instrument repair does not offer any building options, though the nature of the craft requires students to learn how to fabricate individual parts, just not entire instruments.

Q. What are the career goals of students who enter your program?

A. Students who graduate from our program want to get a job repairing musical instruments. They work at music stores that offer repair services or for independent repair shops. Most grads will go out and work in existing repair shops. Some graduates also go into manufacturing for custom builders of musical instruments.

Q. Can you describe a typical day in one of your music labs?

A. For BIR, our labs last from 8:00 A.M. to 3:00 P.M., with 45 minutes for lunch. Typically, one hour is spent demonstrating a skill that students need to acquire. Students spend the balance of their day doing as much real live customer work as they can. BIR has a contract with the Department of Defense to repair its band instruments. When the instruments arrive, students inspect them, do repairs, write up an invoice, and send them back. We try to make the training as much of a real-life experience as possible. With all our repair programs, we focus the training on education for employment.

Q. Are college settings becoming a more popular avenue of training for students?

A. Yes, our nine-month program allows students to get a concentrated education and enter the workforce quickly. Starting salaries for graduates of music instrument repair programs average $20,000 to $25,000, and advance quickly with time and experience. With experience comes the speed necessary to raise one's salary.

Q. **Why are fewer students learning music instrument repair through apprenticeships?**

A. Repair shops, which traditionally offered apprenticeships, are staying busy year-round and are unable to take on apprentices. As a result, many people are opting to go to music instrument repair schools to learn the craft.

This is not to say that apprenticeships are not valuable. The compressed format of instrument repair schools doesn't work for everybody. Apprenticeships last two to three years. Some students learn more effectively through on the-the-job training offered via apprenticeships. One drawback of apprenticeships is that salaries are lower because the apprentice is just learning, not producing for the employer. And employers are not teachers—they do not always have time to give the apprentice the attention he/she requires to advance quickly.

Q. **What personal qualities should a student have to be successful in your program and in their career?**

A. Desire trumps everything. If you think that you're not mechanically inclined to do instrument repair work, don't base your decision on that. Mechanical ability is important but not the quality that matters most to us. Successful students should be determined, have a willingness to learn by doing, and be able to learn from their mistakes. The ability to trade the needs of the ego for the sake of the craft is pivotal and will foster the necessary hand-eye coordination, the ability to concentrate, and the patience required for excellence.

Q. **What advice would you offer students as they complete their degrees and look for jobs?**

A. Regardless of where you go, you are forever a student. A diploma might get you a job, but repair technicians are only successful if they are perpetual learners.

Q. **What is the future of the music instrument repair industry?**

A. We're not immune to economic downturns, but as long as music is part of the American educational framework, there will always be a need for technicians. We have never seen demand for our graduates decline. It is not unusual for the college to have twice as many job offers in our job bank as there are graduates.

One challenge our industry faces is the flood of inexpensive and cheaply made instruments from overseas. Many of these instruments are so poorly made that beginning musicians become frustrated and quit because of instruments that are virtually unplayable out of the shipping box—instruments that are not repairable because they are so poorly constructed. These instruments are now being sold at discounters, on Internet auction sites, and even by retail music stores. How this will impact music education in the schools and the music instrument repair industry remains to be seen. But those of us in the craft remain committed to insuring that the skills of all repair technicians are continually nurtured to assist music educators in fostering the value of music in all people's lives, regardless of age and experience.

Music Conductors and Directors

QUICK FACTS

School Subjects
Music
Theater/dance

Personal Skills
Artistic
Communication/ideas

Work Environment
Primarily indoors
Primarily one location

Minimum Education Level
High school diploma

Salary Range
$15,000 to $40,000 to
$500,000+

Certification or Licensing
None available

Outlook
About as fast as the average

DOT
152

GOE
01.04.01

NOC
5132

O*NET-SOC
27-2041.00, 27-2041.01

OVERVIEW

Music conductors direct large groups of musicians or singers in the performance of a piece of music. There are various types of conductors, including those who lead symphony orchestras, dance bands, marching bands, and choral groups. They use their hands, a baton, or both to indicate the musical sound variations and timing of a composition. Their chief concern is their interpretation of how a piece of music should be played. They are responsible for rehearsing the orchestra and auditioning musicians for positions in the ensemble.

Conductors must have the complete respect of the musicians they lead. The great conductors have a personal charisma that awes both musician and listener alike. Conductors are unique in the modern musical world in that they make no sound themselves yet are able to control the sound that others make. The orchestra is their instrument. Music conductors sometimes carry the title of *music director,* which implies a wider area of responsibilities, including administrative and managerial duties.

HISTORY

The origins of music conducting are not quite clear. Some form of timekeeping undoubtedly went on even among primitive musical groups. In early orchestral days, timekeeping was often done orally, with the use of a scroll, or by pounding a long stick on the floor. During the 18th century, a musician (usually the organist, harpsichordists, or the chief of the first violinists) who often kept time came to be called concertmasters. There were no specialist

A conductor acknowledges applause at the conclusion of a concert. *(Corbis)*

conductors at this time; the composer generally served as the conductor, and he usually conducted only his own works. The concertmaster role grew increasingly important, and for a period it was not unusual for him to keep time by stamping his feet even when there was a separate conductor who might also keep time by clapping his hands or tapping a desk. Needless to say, this simultaneous stamping and clapping could be very irritating to the musicians and audience alike.

The exact date of the introduction of the baton in conducting is not known, but mention of using a staff in this manner was made in Greek mythology in as early as 709 B.C. Batons have been used since the eighth century and became more fashionable as orchestras grew larger in the late 18th century. The baton was at first a rather large and awkward device similar to the instrument used by a drum major. Some conductors eschewed the baton and used a violin bow, a paper scroll, or their bare hands (this last practice was never widely adopted). Early in the 19th century, Ludwig Spohr, perhaps the first musician to be recognized purely as a conductor, was another of the early users of the baton rather than the bow or a paper scroll. By the mid-19th century batons were in wide use.

Early in the history of the orchestra, most concert music was performed in conjunction with opera. In 1816, noted French violinist Rodolphe Kreutzer used his violin bow to conduct the Paris Opera.

In 1824, the Opera employed the services of a specialist conductor, violinist Françoise Antoine Habeneck, who also conducted with a bow, and who in 1828 became one of the first to establish an orchestra devoted entirely to concert as opposed to opera music. Habeneck conducted the first Beethoven symphonies heard in Paris. During these early days of conducting, it was common for the conductor to face the audience rather than the orchestra, a practice that was still common in Russia during the late 19th century.

Another innovation was the use of the full score by conductors. Before the full score was available, conductors usually read from the first violinist's part. Berlioz was one of the first to employ the full score and was one of the great 19th-century composer-conductors who influenced conducting style into the next century. Among the other major influences were Felix Mendelssohn and Richard Wagner. These men assumed full, autocratic command of the orchestra, each insisting on strict obedience from the musicians in carrying out the conductor's interpretation of the music. Each developed his own characteristic style, which brought him widespread adulation. Berlioz had an inspirational effect on the orchestra and, while his physical style was flamboyant, he was rather inflexible in his tempo. Mendelssohn was also strict in his timing, while Wagner took a more flexible approach.

Among the conductors influenced by Wagner were such notable figures as Hans von Bulow, Franz Liszt, and Wilhelm Furtwangler. Mendelssohn's followers included Karl Muck, Felix Weingartner, and Richard Strauss, all distinctive for their minimal baton movement and methodical tempos. Some conductors defied categorization, however. One of these was Gustav Mahler in the late 19th century; he wielded a tyrannical power over the orchestra and flew into rages that became legendary.

Many different conducting styles emerged in the 20th century, including some that were highly exhibitionistic. One of the extremes of that type was exemplified by Sir Thomas Beecham, the great British conductor. He sometimes raised his arms skyward, imploring the orchestra to reach for perfection; at other times he lunged at the horn section to raise its power, occasionally falling off the podium in his excitement. Leopold Stokowski and Leonard Bernstein have also been noted for their dramatic exhibitionism. In the early 1920s in Russia, an attempt was made at forming a conductorless orchestra. The experiment died out after a few years, although in the late 1920s conductorless experiments were attempted in New York City and Budapest.

The outstanding conductors in the 20th century are too numerous to mention, but one name is perhaps legendary above all others:

Arturo Toscanini. Originally an opera composer, his infallible ear, musicianship, comprehensive knowledge of scores, and orchestral control made him virtually the prototype of great 20th century conductors. At rehearsals his famed temper flared as he exhorted his charges to perfectly perform his interpretation of a score. Before the audience he exuded charisma. Toscanini, who conducted the New York Philharmonic-Symphony from 1928 to 1936 and the NBC Symphony from 1937 to 1954, was perhaps the most influential conductor of the mid-20th century, his main rival being Furtwangler in Germany. Some conductors of the late 20th century, however, remained free of both influences. Perhaps the most notable of these is Sir Georg Solti, who, with large and seemingly awkward movements, inspired his musicians to brilliant heights of musical perfection. Many authorities acknowledge that under his guidance the Chicago Symphony Orchestra became one of the finest musical ensembles of the late 20th century. While many women have taken their places among the great orchestras of the world, few have been able to move into the field of conducting. In the second half of the 20th century, however, there were some breakthroughs, and a number of women conductors, such as Sarah Caldwell in the United States, achieved notable recognition.

THE JOB

Conducting, whether it be of a symphony orchestra, an opera, a chorus, a theater pit orchestra, a marching band, or even a big swing band, is an enormously complex and demanding occupation to which only the exceptional individual can possibly aspire with hope of even moderate success. Music conductors must have multiple skills and talents. First and foremost, they must be consummate musicians. Not only should they have mastered an instrument, but they also must know music and be able to interpret the score of any composition. They should have an unerring ear and a bearing that commands the respect of the musicians. Conductors need to be sensitive to the musicians, sympathetic to their problems, and able to inspire them to bring out the very best they have to offer. Conductors must also have a sense of showmanship. Some conductors have advanced farther than others because their dramatic conducting style helps bring in larger audiences and greater receipts. The conductor must also be a psychologist who can deal with the multiplicity of complex and temperamental personalities presented by a large ensemble of musicians and singers. Conductors must exude personal charm; orchestras are always fundraising, and the conductor is frequently expected to meet major donors to keep their goodwill. Finally, and in line with fund-raising, music conductors and directors are expected to have administrative skills and to understand the business and financial problems that face the orchestra organization.

Conductors are distinguished by their baton technique and arm and body movements. These can vary widely from conductor to conductor, some being reserved and holding to minimal movements, others using sweeping baton strokes and broad arm and body gestures. There is no right or wrong way to conduct; it is a highly individualized art, and great conductors produce excellent results using contrasting styles. The conductor's fundamental purpose in leading, regardless of style, is to set the tempo and rhythm of a piece. Conductors must be sure that the orchestra is following their interpretation of the music, and they must resolve any problems that the score poses. The conductor often receives the blame when a composition fails to render a composition in a way that is pleasing to the public and the critics.

The quality of a performance is probably most directly related to the conductor's rehearsal techniques. During rehearsals conductors must diagnose and correct to their satisfaction the musical, interpretive, rhythmic, balance, and intonation problems the orchestra encounters. They must work with each unit of the orchestra individually and the entire ensemble as a whole; this may include soloist instrumentalists and singers as well as a chorus. Some conductors rehearse every detail of a score while others have been known to emphasize only certain parts during rehearsal. Some are quiet and restrained at rehearsals, while others work to a feverish emotional pitch. The sound that an orchestra makes is also identified with the conductor, and for some, such as Eugene Ormandy, formerly conductor of the Philadelphia Orchestra, the tone of an orchestra becomes a recognizable signature. Tone is determined by the conductor's use of the various sections of the orchestra. The brass section, for instance, can be instructed to play so that the sound is bright, sharp, and piercing, or they can play to produce a rich, sonorous, and heavy sound. The strings can play the vibrato broadly to produce a thick, lush tone or play with little vibrato to produce a thinner, more delicate sound.

REQUIREMENTS

High School

Formal training in at least one musical instrument is necessary for a future as a music conductor or director. Keyboard instruction is particularly important. In high school, participation in a concert band, jazz ensemble, choir, or orchestra will teach you about group performing and how the various parts contribute to a whole sound. Some high schools may offer opportunities to conduct school music groups.

Postsecondary Training

It is unlikely that many people start out at a very early point in life to become a music conductor. Most conductors begin studying music at an early age and possibly, at some later, more mature point of life may discover or suspect that they have the qualities to become a conductor. Some people become involved with conducting at the high school or college level, leading a small group for whom they may also do the arranging and possibly some composing. There are some courses specifically in conducting at advanced institutions, and interested students may take courses in composition, arranging, and orchestrating, which provide a good background for conducting. Some opportunities to conduct may arise in the university, and you may be able to study with a faculty member who conducts the school orchestra. There are also conductor training programs and apprenticeship programs, which are announced in the music trade papers.

It was once commonly thought that conducting was unteachable. That attitude has been changing, however, and some institutions have developed formalized programs to teach the art of conducting. The Paris Conservatory is particularly noted for its conducting instruction. The Julliard School in New York is another institution known for its studies in conducting.

Conductors must acquire multiple skills in order to practice their art. These skills may be divided into three parts: technical, performance, and conducting.

Technical skills deal with conductors' ability to control orchestral intonation, balance, and color; they must be advanced at sight reading and transposition in order to cope with orchestral scores. Conductors must acquire a comprehensive knowledge of all orchestral instruments and must have mastery of at least one instrument, the piano probably being the most helpful. They must acquire skills in composition and music analysis, which presumes accomplished skills in counterpoint, harmony, musical structures, and orchestration. Finally, conductors must understand and be able to adapt musical styling.

Performance skills refer to conductors' own instrumental ability. Mastery of one instrument is important, but the more instruments conductors know, the better they will be able to relate to members of the orchestra. It is through knowledge of instruments that conductors develop their interpretive abilities.

Conducting skills involve the ability to use the baton and to control the timing, rhythm, and structure of a musical piece. Conductors must develop these skills at performances and at rehearsals. At rehearsals they must use their power and their intellect to blend the various elements of the orchestra and the composition into a single unified presentation. Conductors must also learn to use their whole bodies, along with the baton, to control the music.

Conductors require not only an extensive knowledge of music but also a strong general background in the arts and humanities. They should have a comprehensive knowledge of musical history as it fits into the general fabric of civilization along with competence in various languages, including French, German, Italian, and Latin. Language skills are particularly helpful in coaching singers. Familiarity with the history of Western civilization, particularly its literature, drama, and art, will also be valuable in the composer's musical frame of reference.

Other Requirements

Conductors require a high degree of self-discipline and unquestioned integrity in order to fill a difficult and complex leadership role. It is important as well that they learn all the aspects of the business and social functions of an orchestra.

Like musicians and composers, conductors must have talent, a quality that cannot be taught or acquired. They must have supreme self-confidence in their ability to lead and interpret the music of the great masters. They must convince both audience and ensemble that they are in command.

EXPLORING

The best way to become familiar with the art of conducting is to study music and the great conductors themselves. It is not possible to understand conducting beyond the most superficial level without a good background in music. Students of conducting should go to as many musical presentations as they can, such as symphonies, operas, and musical theater, and study the conductors, noting their baton techniques and their arm and body movements. Try to determine how the orchestra and audience respond to the gesturing of the conductors. There are also many associations, reference books, and biographies that provide detailed information about conductors and their art. One of the most prominent organizations is the American Symphony

Orchestra League located in Washington, D.C. It holds a national conference and conducting workshops each year.

EMPLOYERS

Conductors and directors work in many contexts. Music teachers in schools often take on conducting as a natural extension of their duties. Conservatories and institutions of higher learning frequently have fine orchestras, choruses, and bands that often choose conductors from the faculty. There are numerous summer festivals that employ conductors, and conductors may also find positions with community orchestras and choruses, local opera companies, and musical theater groups; even amateur groups sometimes hire outside conductors. For the very exceptional, of course, there is the possibility of conducting with famous orchestras, theaters, and opera companies, as well as the musical groups associated with broadcasting and film studios. Well-known conductors are in demand and travel a great deal, appearing as guest conductors with other orchestras or making personal appearances.

STARTING OUT

A career in conducting begins with a sound musical education. Working as an instrumentalist in an orchestral group under a good conductor whose technique can be studied is an important step toward conducting. The piano is an important instrument for conductors to know, because it will not only enable them to score and arrange more easily, it also will be useful in coaching singers, which many conductors do as a sideline, and in rehearsing an orchestra as an assistant conductor. That is not to say, however, that other instrumentalists do not also acquire a good background for conducting.

With a solid foundation in musical education and some experience with an orchestra, young conductors should seek any way possible to acquire conducting experience. There are many grants and fellowships you can apply for, and many summer music festivals advertise for conductors. These situations often present the opportunity to work or study under a famous conductor who has been engaged to oversee or administer a festival. Such experience is invaluable because it provides opportunities to make contacts for other conducting positions. These may include apprenticeships, jobs with university choirs and orchestras (which may include a faculty position), or opportunities with community orchestras, small opera companies, or amateur groups that seek a professional music director. Experience in these positions can lead to offers with major orchestras, operas, or musical theater companies as an assistant or associate conductor.

Not everyone will want or be able to move into a major role as a conductor of a well-known orchestra. Many, in fact most, will remain in other positions such as those described. Those seeking to further their career as a conductor may want to invest in a personal manager who will find bookings and situations for ambitious young talent. More than likely, entering the conducting field will take more of an investment than most other careers. Music education, applying for grants and fellowships, and attending workshops, summer music camps, and festivals can add up to a considerable expense. Moving into a good conducting job may take time as well, and young people going into the field should not expect to reach the pinnacle of their profession until they are well into their 30s or 40s or even older.

ADVANCEMENT

There is no real hierarchy in an orchestra organization that one can climb to the role of conductor. The most likely advancement within an organization would be from the position of assistant or associate conductor or from that of the head first violinist, that is, the concertmaster. Conductors generally move from smaller conducting jobs to larger ones. A likely advancement would be from a small community orchestra or youth orchestra (probably a part-time position), to a small city orchestra (full or part time), and from there to a larger city orchestra, a mid-sized opera company, or directorship of a middle-level television or film company. Such advancement presumes that the conductor has had sufficient recognition and quality reviews to come to the attention of the larger musical groups.

Conductors who take the leadership of mid-sized city orchestras and opera companies may be in the hands of an agent or manager who takes care of financial matters, guest bookings, and personal appearances. The agent will also be looking for advancement to more prestigious conducting jobs in the larger cities. At the point that conductors receive national or international recognition, it becomes a question of which major position they will accept as openings occur. It is unlikely that a major city's orchestra would promote someone within the organization when the conductorship is open. It is more probable that a search committee will conduct an international search to find a big name conductor for the post. Conductors themselves can advance to top-level administrative positions, such as artistic director or executive director.

EARNINGS

The range of earnings for music conductors and directors is enormous, and there is variation from one category of conductors to another. For instance, many conductors work only part time and make small yearly incomes for their conducting endeavors. Part-time choir directors for churches and temples, for instance, make from $3,500 to $25,000 per year, while full-time directors make from $15,000 to $40,000 per year. Conductors of dance bands make from $300 to $1,200 per week. Opera and choral group conductors make as little as $8,000 per year working part-time at the community level, but salaries range to over $100,000 per year for those with permanent positions with established companies in major cities. The same applies to symphony orchestra conductors who, for instance, make $25,000 to $40,000 per year conducting smaller, regional orchestras, but who can make $500,000 or more a year if they become the resident conductor of an internationally famous orchestra.

WORK ENVIRONMENT

The working conditions of conductors range as widely as their earnings. The conductors of small musical groups at the community level may rehearse in a member's basement, a community center, a high school gym, or in a church or temple. Performances may be held in some of those same places. Lighting, heating or cooling, sound equipment, and musical instrument quality may all be less than adequate. On the other hand, conductors of major orchestras in the larger metropolitan centers usually have ideal working conditions, generally having the same outstanding facilities for rehearsal and performance. Many universities, colleges, and conservatories, even some of the smaller ones, also have state-of-the-art facilities.

OUTLOOK

The operating cost for an orchestra continues to grow every year, and music organizations are in constant budget-trimming modes as have been most other professional business organizations in the last decade. This has tended to affect growth in the orchestra field and, accordingly, the number of conducting jobs. Additionally, the overall number of orchestras in the United States has grown only slightly in the last two decades. The number of orchestras in academia declined slightly while community, youth, and city orchestras for the most part increased slightly in number. The slight growth pattern of orchestra groups will not nearly accommodate the number of people who graduated from music school during that period and are trying to become conductors. The competition for music conductor and director jobs, already tight, will become even tighter in the next decade. Only the most talented people moving into the field will be able to find full-time jobs.

FOR MORE INFORMATION

For information on membership in the local union nearest you, contact
American Federation of Musicians of the United States and Canada
1501 Broadway, Suite 600
New York, NY 10036
http://www.afm.org

For information on membership, contact
American Guild of Musical Artists
1430 Broadway, 14th Floor
New York, NY 10018
Tel: 212-265-3687
http://www.musicalartists.org

For information on scholarships, orchestra management careers, and job listings, contact
American Symphony Orchestra League
33 West 60th Street, 5th Floor
New York, NY 10023
Tel: 212-262-5161
http://www.symphony.org

For information on membership and the Guild's mentoring program, contact
Conductors' Guild, Inc.
5300 Glenside Drive, Suite 2207
Richmond, VA 23228
Tel: 804-553-1378
http://www.conductorsguild.org

For information on auditions and competitions in Canada, contact
Orchestras Canada
56 The Esplanade, Suite 203
Toronto, ON M5E 1A7 Canada
Tel: 416-366-8834
http://www.oc.ca

Musicians

OVERVIEW

Musicians perform, compose, conduct, arrange, and teach music. Performing musicians may work alone or as part of a group, or ensemble. They may play before live audiences in clubs or auditoriums, or they may perform on television or radio, in motion pictures, or in a recording studio. Musicians usually play either classical, popular (including rock and country), jazz, or folk music, but many musicians play several musical styles. Musicians, singers, and related workers hold approximately 240,000 jobs in the United States.

HISTORY

According to ancient art and artifacts, humankind has enjoyed music at least since the establishment of early civilizations in the Tigris-Euphrates Valley. Musicians of these early cultures played instruments that were blown, plucked, or struck, just as is done by the musicians of today. Most of the early music, however, was vocal. In the ancient Egyptian temples, choirs sang to honor the gods, while in the court, musicians accompanied their songs with instruments of the wind, string, and percussion families. The ancient tribes of Israel used a shofar (a ram's horn trumpet) to accompany some religious services, a practice that has been continued to the present day. It was the development of music in Greece, however, that clearly influenced Western music. The Greeks had a system of writing their music down, and they invented a system of scales called modes that was the forerunner of the modern major and minor scales. Roman music was founded on the Greek model. A seven-tone scale evolved under the Romans, and instrumentation was further developed, including the straight trumpet.

During the Middle Ages, a great catalyst for both change and preservation in music arrived with the development of musical notation, the written language of music. Much credit for this accomplishment is ascribed to Guido d'Arezzo, an 11th-century Italian monk who devised a system for writing music down on paper so that it might be preserved and later read and played by other musicians. Many monks during this period devoted their lives to the preservation of the music of the Church, and much of the knowledge and development of music is owed to their dedicated efforts. Throughout the Middle Ages, singers and musicians traveled from town to town to play for new audiences. During the Renaissance, singers and musicians often had to depend on wealthy patrons for support. What we now call classical music developed during the Renaissance.

During the 17th century, the operatic form developed, most notably in Italy. Opera, combining orchestral music and theater with an extremely popular form of singing, opened up a whole new range of opportunities for musicians, particularly singers. Singers soon began to gain fame in their own right for their incredible vocal feats, and great public demand for their performances allowed them to sever their dependent ties to wealthy patrons.

From about the mid-18th century to the mid-19th century, opportunities for instrumental musicians expanded as composers began to write more complex musical pieces for larger ensembles. During this period, many of the world's great symphonies, concerti, and chamber music were written and performed by musicians playing an ever-widening array of instruments. In the early 1800s came the onset of the Romantic movement in music, in which composers wrote with a new degree of emotionalism and self-expression that conductors and musicians were expected to express in their performance. Around the beginning of the 20th century, musical performers faced another challenge as composers, seeking to break new musical ground, adapted atonal and discordant sounds and new rhythms to their compositions, a direction greatly influenced by the 12-tone scale of Arnold Schoenberg.

The operatic, classical, and nationalistic music of Europe was brought to America by migrating Europeans. Throughout the early history of the United States, virtually all of the music played was European in style. By the end of the 19th century, however, and through the 20th, musicians increasingly came to play music that was distinctly American in style and composition. At least one musical form, jazz, was entirely an American invention.

The development of popular music and the development of recorded music greatly increased opportunities for musicians. U.S.

popular music and jazz influenced music throughout the world. Swing grew out of jazz, and big swing bands mushroomed all over the United States during the late 1930s, 1940s, and into the 1950s. Big bands diminished by the late 1950s as rising costs and new popular music styles, such as rhythm and blues and rock and roll, directed the move to smaller groups using electric and electronic instruments. With the advent of electronic mass media, the musical superstar was created, as millions of people at a time could hear and see musical performers. Although the mass electronic media created an enormous market for popular music, it has ironically limited the market for live performances by musicians. The demand for live musicians was also reduced by the widening use of advanced electronic instruments, such as the synthesizer, which itself can replace a whole band, and the DJ (disc jockey), who plays recorded music over highly sophisticated sound systems, replacing musicians at clubs and gatherings.

Until about the mid-1900s, musicians and singers were largely an exploited group who made little money for the use of their skills. The growth of organizations designed to protect performing artists has helped greatly to improve the lot of musicians. Particularly effective was the American Federation of Musicians, the musicians' union, which created a wage scale and oversaw the rights of musicians in recording, broadcasting, theater, and at any event in which musicians or their recordings are used. In some situations the union requires that live musicians be hired.

THE JOB

Instrumental musicians play one or more musical instruments, usually in a group and in some cases as featured soloists. Musical instruments are usually classified in several distinct categories according to the method by which they produce sound: strings (violins, cellos, basses, etc.), which make sounds by vibrations from bowing or plucking; woodwinds (oboes, clarinets, saxophones), which make sounds by air vibrations through reeds; brass (trumpets, French horns, trombones, etc.), which make sounds by air vibrations through metal; and percussion (drums, pianos, triangles), which produce sound by striking. Instruments can also be classified as electric or acoustic, especially in popular music. Synthesizers are another common instrument, and computer and other electronic technology increasingly is used for creating music.

Like other instrumental musicians, *singers* use their own voice as an instrument to convey music. They aim to express emotion through lyric phrasing and characterization.

Musicians may play in symphony orchestras, dance bands, jazz bands, rock bands, country bands, or other groups or they might go it alone. Some musicians may play in recording studios either with their group or as a session player for a particular recording. Recordings are in the form of records, tapes, compact discs, videotape cassettes, and digital video discs. *Classical musicians* perform in concerts, opera performances, and chamber music concerts, and they may also play in theater orchestras, although theater music is not normally classical. The most talented ones may work as soloists with orchestras or alone in recitals. Some classical musicians accompany singers and choirs, and they may also perform in churches, temples, and other religious settings.

Musicians who play popular music make heavy use of such rhythm instruments as piano, bass, drums, and guitar. *Jazz musicians* also feature woodwind and brass instruments, especially the saxophone and trumpet, and they extensively utilize the bass. Synthesizers are also commonly used jazz instruments; some music is performed entirely on synthesizers, which can be programmed to imitate a variety of instruments and sounds. Musicians in jazz, blues, country, and rock groups play clubs, festivals, and concert halls and may perform music for recordings, television, and motion picture sound tracks. Occasionally they appear in a movie themselves. Other musicians compose, record, and perform entirely with electronic instruments, such as synthesizers and other devices. In the late 1970s, *rap artists* began using turntables as musical instruments, and later, samplers, which record a snippet of other songs and sounds, as part of their music.

Instrumental musicians and singers use their skills to convey the form and meaning of written music. They work to achieve precision, fluency, and emotion within a piece of music, whether through an instrument or through their own voices. Musicians practice constantly to perfect their techniques.

Many musicians supplement their incomes through teaching, while others teach as their full-time occupation, perhaps playing jobs occasionally. *Voice and instrumental music teachers* work in colleges, high schools, elementary schools, conservatories, and in their own studios; often they give concerts and recitals featuring their students. Many professional musicians give private lessons. Students learn to read music, develop their voices, breathe correctly, and hold their instruments properly.

Choral directors lead groups of singers in schools and other organizations. Church choirs, community oratorio societies, and professional symphony choruses are among the groups that employ choral directors outside of school settings. Choral directors audition singers, select music, and direct singers in achieving the tone, variety, intensity, and phrasing that they feel is required. *Orchestra conductors* do the same with instrumental musicians. Many work in schools and smaller communities, but the best conduct large orchestras in major cities. Some are resident instructors, while others travel constantly, making guest appearances with major national and foreign orchestras. They are responsible for the overall sound and quality of their orchestras.

Individuals also write and prepare music for themselves or other musicians to play and sing. *Composers* write the original music for symphonies, songs, or operas using musical notation to express their ideas through melody, rhythm, and harmony. *Arrangers* and *orchestrators* take a composer's work and transcribe it for the various orchestra sections or individual instrumentalists and singers to perform; they prepare music for film scores, musical theater, television, or recordings. *Copyists* assist composers and arrangers by copying down the various parts of a composition, each of which is played by a different section of the orchestra. *Librettists* write words to opera and musical theater scores, and *lyricists* write words to songs and other short musical pieces. A number of *songwriters* compose both music and lyrics, and many are musicians who perform their own songs.

REQUIREMENTS

High School

If you are interested in becoming a musician, you will probably have begun to develop your musical skills long before you entered high school. While you are in high school, however, there are a number of classes you can take that will help you broaden your knowledge. Naturally, take band, orchestra, or choir classes, depending on your interest. In addition, you should also take mathematics classes, since any musician needs to understand counting, rhythms, and beats. Many professional musicians write at least some of their own music, and a strong math background is very helpful for this. If your high school offers courses in music history or appreciation, be sure to take these. Finally, take classes such as English and psychology that will improve your communication skills and your understanding of people and emotions. If you are interested in working in the classical music field, you will most likely need a college degree to succeed in this area. Therefore, be sure to round out your high school education by taking other college preparatory classes. Finally, no matter what type of musician you want to be, you will need to devote much of your after-school time to your private study and practice of music.

Postsecondary Training

Depending on your interest, especially if it is popular music, further formal education is not required. College or conservatory degrees are only required for those who plan to teach in institutions. Nevertheless, you will only benefit from continued education.

Scores of colleges and universities have excellent music schools, and there are numerous conservatories that offer degrees in music. Many schools have noted musicians on their staff, and music students often have the advantage of studying under a professor who has a distinguished career in music. By studying with someone like this, you will not only learn more about music and performance, but you will also begin to make valuable connections in the field. You should know that having talent and a high grade point average do not always ensure entry into the top music schools. Competition for positions is extremely tough. You will probably have to audition, and only the most talented are accepted.

College undergraduates in music school generally take courses in music theory, harmony, counterpoint, rhythm, melody, ear training, applied music, and music history. Courses in composing, arranging, and conducting are available in most comprehensive music schools. Students will also have to take courses such as English and psychology along with a regular academic program.

Certification or Licensing

Musicians who want to teach in state elementary and high schools must be state certified. To obtain a state certificate, musicians must satisfactorily complete a degree-granting course in music education at an institution of higher learning. About 600 institutions in the United States offer programs in music education that qualify students for state certificates. Music education programs include many of the same courses mentioned earlier for musicians in general. They also include education courses and supervised practice teaching. To teach in colleges and universities or in conservatories generally requires a graduate degree in music. Widely recognized musicians, however, sometimes receive positions in higher education without having obtained a degree.

The American Guild of Organists offers a number of voluntary, professional certifications to its members. Visit the Guild's website (http://www.agohq.org) for more information.

Other Requirements

Hard work and dedication are key factors in a musical career, but music is an art form, and like those who practice any of the fine arts, musicians will succeed according to the amount of musical talent they have. Those who have talent and are willing to make sacrifices to develop it are the ones most likely to succeed. How much talent and ability one has is always open to speculation and opinion, and it may take years of studying and practice before musicians can assess their own limitations.

There are other requirements necessary to becoming a professional musician that are just as important as training, education, and study. Foremost among these is a love of music strong enough to endure the arduous training and working life of a musician. To become an accomplished musician and to be recognized in the field requires an uncommon degree of dedication, self-discipline, and drive. Musicians who would move ahead must practice constantly with a determination to improve their technique and quality of performance. Musicians also need to develop an emotional toughness that will help them deal with rejection, indifference to their work, and ridicule from critics, which will be especially prevalent early in their careers. There is also praise and adulation along the way, which is easier to take but also requires a certain psychological handling.

For musicians interested in careers in popular music, little to no formal training is necessary. Many popular musicians teach themselves to play their instruments, which often results in the creation of new and exciting playing styles. Quite often, popular musicians do not even know how to read music. Some would say that many rock musicians do not even know how to play their instruments. This was especially true in the early days of the punk era (c. late 1970s-early 1980s). Most musicians, however, have a natural talent for rhythm and melody.

Many musicians often go through years of paying their dues—that is, receiving little money, respect, or attention for their efforts. Therefore, they must have a strong sense of commitment to their careers and to their creative ideas.

Professional musicians generally hold membership in the American Federation of Musicians, and concert soloists also hold membership in the American Guild of Musical Artists, Inc. Singers can belong to a branch of Associated Actors and Artists of America. Music teachers in schools often hold membership in MENC: The National Association for Music Education.

EXPLORING

The first step to exploring your interest in a musical career is to become involved with music. Elementary schools, high schools, and institutions of higher education all present a number of options for musical training and performance, including choirs, ensembles,

Job Tips

Finding a job as a professional musician can be daunting. There are hundreds of thousands of musicians and singers out there competing with you for top jobs. The American Federation of Music offers the following advice to aspiring musicians trying to break into the business:

- If you live in a small town and can't seem to get any gigs, consider moving to a larger town or city where you'll have better and more diverse job opportunities.

- To get experience, offer your services for free at charity events, town celebrations, political fundraisers, and corporate events. This will help you get your foot (or saxophone) in the door and expose you to large groups of people who might eventually offer you paying jobs.

- Work as a musician or singer at your local church, synagogue, or mosque. Whether you are paid for your performance or not, this type of employment can provide steady work, help you hone your performance skills, and, again, introduce your talents to a large group of potential customers.

- Create a CD of your best work and send it to radio stations, record companies, and potential clients.

- Think of work settings beyond clubs and concert halls. Cruise ships and amusement parks often hire musicians to entertain people. You might also try to land work as a musician in the television and radio advertising industries.

- Learn to play multiple instruments or perform in a variety of musical genres. This will make you more attractive to a wider variety of clients and employers.

- If you have a good personality, excellent music skills, and have a desire to travel, consider working as a product specialist for a music instrument manufacturer. Product specialists hold clinics at retail music stores to educate salespeople and consumers about an instrument's benefits and features.

- If you are having trouble hitting the right notes in your search for musician gigs, consider teaching in your local community or at the college level. Teaching others is a demanding, but rewarding, alternative to music performance. It is also a great way to network and meet people who might be able to help you find jobs as a musician.

bands, and orchestras. You also may have chances to perform in school musicals and talent shows. Those involved with services at churches, synagogues, or other religious institutions have excellent opportunities for exploring their interest in music. If you can afford to, take private music lessons.

Besides learning more about music, you will most likely have the chance to play in recitals arranged by your teacher. You may also want to attend special summer camps or programs that focus on the field. Interlochen Center for the Arts (http://www.interlochen.org), for example, offers summer camps for students from the elementary to the high school level. College, university, and conservatory students gain valuable performance experience by appearing in recitals and playing in bands, orchestras, and school shows. The more enterprising students in high school and in college form their own bands and begin earning money by playing while still in school.

It is important for you to take advantage of every opportunity to audition so that you become comfortable with this process. There are numerous community amateur and semiprofessional theater groups throughout the United States that produce musical plays and operettas, in which beginning musicians can gain playing experience.

EMPLOYERS

Most musicians work in large urban areas and are particularly drawn to the major recording centers, such as Chicago, New York City, Los Angeles, Nashville, and Miami Beach. Most musicians find work in churches, temples, schools, clubs, restaurants, and cruise lines, at weddings, in opera and ballet productions, and on film, television, and radio. Religious organizations are the largest single source of work for musicians.

Full-time positions as a musician in a choir, symphony orchestra, or band are few and are held only by the most talented. Musicians who are versatile and willing to work hard will find a variety of opportunities available, but all musicians should understand that work is not likely to be steady or provide much security. Many musicians support themselves in another line of work while pursuing their musical careers on a part-time basis. Busy musicians often hire agents to find employers and negotiate contracts or conditions of employment.

STARTING OUT

Young musicians need to get involved in as many playing situations as they can in their school and community musical groups. They

should audition as often as possible, because experience at auditioning is very important. Whenever possible, they should take part in
seminars and internships offered by orchestras, colleges, and associations. The National Orchestral Association offers training programs
for musicians who want a career in the orchestral field.

Musicians who want to perform with established groups, such as
choirs and symphony orchestras, enter the field by auditioning.
Recommendations from teachers and other musicians often help
would-be musicians obtain the opportunity to audition. Concert and
opera soloists are also required to audition. Musicians must prepare
themselves thoroughly for these auditions, which are demanding and
stressful. A bad audition can be very discouraging for the young
musician.

Popular musicians often begin playing at low-paying social functions and at small clubs or restaurants. If people like their performances, they usually move on to bookings at larger rooms in better
clubs. Continued success leads to a national reputation and possible
recording contracts. Jazz musicians tend to operate in the same way,
taking every opportunity to audition with established jazz musicians.

Music teachers enter the field by applying directly to schools.
College and university placement offices often have listings of positions. Professional associations frequently list teaching openings in
their newsletters and journals, as do newspapers. Music-oriented
journals—such as the American Federation of Musicians' journal
International Musician (http://www.afm.org/public/musicbiz/
intmus.php)—are excellent sources to check for job listings.

ADVANCEMENT

Popular musicians, once they have become established with a band,
advance by moving up to more famous bands or by taking leadership
of their own group. Bands may advance from playing small clubs to
larger halls and even stadiums and festivals. They may receive a
recording contract; if their songs or recordings prove successful, they
can command higher fees for their contracts. Symphony orchestra
musicians advance by moving to the head of their section of the
orchestra. They can also move up to a position such as assistant or
associate conductor. Once instrumental musicians acquire a reputation as accomplished artists, they receive engagements that are of
higher status and remuneration, and they may come into demand as
soloists. As their reputations develop, both classical and popular
musicians may receive attractive offers to make recordings and personal appearances.

Popular and opera singers move up to better and more lucrative jobs through recognition of their talent by the public or by music producers and directors and agents. Their advancement is directly related to the demand for their talent and their own ability to promote themselves.

Music teachers in elementary and secondary schools may, with further training, aspire to careers as supervisors of music of a school system, a school district, or an entire state. With further graduate training, teachers can qualify for positions in colleges, universities, and music conservatories, where they can advance to become department heads. Well-known musicians can become artists-in-residence in the music departments of institutions of higher learning.

EARNINGS

It is difficult to estimate the earnings of the average musician, because what a musician earns is dependent upon his or her skill, reputation, geographic location, type of music, and number of engagements per year.

According to the American Federation of Musicians, musicians in the major U.S. symphony orchestras earned salaries of between $24,720 and $100,196 during the 2000–01 performance season. The season for these major orchestras, generally located in the largest U.S. cities, ranges from 24 to 52 weeks. Featured musicians and soloists can earn much more, especially those with an international reputation. According to the U.S. Department of Labor, median annual earnings of musicians, singers, and related workers were $36,290 in 2002.

Popular musicians are usually paid per concert or gig. A band just starting out playing a small bar or club may be required to play three sets a night, and each musician may receive next to nothing for the entire evening. Often, bands receive a percentage of the cover charge at the door. Some musicians play for drinks alone. On average, however, pay per musician ranges from $30 to $300 or more per night. Bands that have gained recognition and a following may earn far more, because a club owner can usually be assured that many people will come to see the band play. The most successful popular musicians, of course, can earn millions of dollars each year. By the end of the 1990s, some artists, in fact, had signed recording contracts worth $20 million or more.

Musicians are well paid for studio recording work, when they can get it. For recording film and television background music, musicians are paid a minimum of about $185 for a three-hour session; for record company recordings they receive a minimum of about $235 for three hours. Instrumentalists performing live earn anywhere from $30 to $300 per engagement, depending on their degree of popularity, talent, and the size of the room they play.

According to the American Guild of Organists, full-time organists employed by religious institutions had the following base salary ranges by educational attainment in 2003: bachelor's degree, $45,253 to $64,356; master's degree, $51,486 to $74,256; and Ph.D., $58,001 to $83,584.

The salaries received by music teachers in public elementary and secondary schools are the same as for other teachers. According to the U.S. Department of Labor, public elementary and high school teachers had median yearly earnings of $41,780 and $43,950, respectively, in 2002. Music teachers in colleges and universities have widely ranging salaries. Most teachers supplement their incomes through private instruction and by performing in their off hours.

Most musicians do not, as a rule, work steadily for one employer, and they often undergo long periods of unemployment between engagements. Because of these factors, few musicians can qualify for unemployment compensation. Unlike other workers, most musicians also do not enjoy such benefits as sick leave or paid vacations. Some musicians, on the other hand, who work under contractual agreements, do receive benefits, which usually have been negotiated by artists unions, such as the American Federation of Musicians.

WORK ENVIRONMENT

Work conditions for musicians vary greatly. Performing musicians generally work in the evenings and on weekends. They also spend much time practicing and rehearsing for performances. Their workplace can be almost anywhere, from a swanky club to a high school gymnasium to a dark, dingy bar. Many concerts are given outdoors and in a variety of weather conditions. Performers may be given a star's dressing room, share a mirror in a church basement, or have to change in a bar's storeroom. They may work under the hot camera lights of film or television sets or tour with a troupe in subzero temperatures. They may work amid the noise and confusion of a large rehearsal of a Broadway show or in the relative peace and quiet of a small recording studio. Seldom are two days in a performer's life just alike.

Many musicians and singers travel a great deal. More prominent musicians may travel with staffs who make their arrangements and take care of wardrobes and equipment. Their accommodations are usually quite comfortable, if not luxurious, and they generally play in major urban centers. Lesser-known musicians may have to take care of all their own arrangements and put up with modest accommodations in relatively remote places. Some musicians perform on the streets, at subway or bus stations, and other places likely to have a great deal of passersby. Symphony orchestra musicians probably travel less than most, but musicians in major orchestras usually travel first class.

The chief characteristic of musical employment is its lack of continuity. Few musicians work full time and most experience periods of unemployment between engagements. Most work day jobs to supplement their music or performing incomes. Those who are in great demand generally have agents and managers to help direct their careers.

Music teachers affiliated with institutions work the same hours as other classroom teachers. Many of these teachers, however, spend time after school and on weekends directing and instructing school vocal and instrumental groups. Teachers may also have varied working conditions. They may teach in a large urban school, conducting five different choruses each day, or they may work in several rural elementary schools and spend much time driving from school to school.

College or university instructors may divide their time between group and individual instruction. They may teach several musical subjects and may be involved with planning and producing school musical events. They may also supervise student music teachers when they do their practice teaching.

Private music teachers work part or full time out of their own homes or in separate studios. The ambiance of their workplace would be in accordance with the size and nature of their clientele.

OUTLOOK

It is difficult to make a living solely as a musician, and this will continue because competition for jobs will be as intense as it has been in the past. Most musicians must hold down other jobs while pursuing their music careers. Thousands of musicians are all trying to make it in the music industry. Musicians are advised to be as versatile as possible, playing various kinds of music and more than one instrument. More importantly, they must be committed to pursuing their craft.

The U.S. Department of Labor predicts that employment of musicians will grow about as fast as the average over the next several years. The demand for musicians will be greatest in theaters, bands, and restaurants as the public continues to spend more money on recreational activities. The outlook is favorable in churches and other religious organizations. The increasing numbers of cable television networks and new television programs will likely cause an increase in employment for musicians. Digital recording technology has also made it easier and less expensive for musicians to produce and distribute their own recordings. However, few musicians will earn substantial incomes from these efforts. Popular musicians may receive many short-term engagements in nightclubs, restaurants, and theaters, but these engagements offer little job stability. The supply of musicians for virtually all types of music will continue to exceed the demand for the foreseeable future.

FOR MORE INFORMATION

For information on membership in a local union nearest you, developments in the music field, a searchable database of U.S. and foreign music schools, and articles on careers in music, visit the following website:
American Federation of Musicians of the United States and
Canada
1501 Broadway, Suite 600
New York, NY 10036
Tel: 212-869-1330
http://www.afm.org

The AGMA is a union for professional musicians. The website has information on upcoming auditions, news announcements for the field, and membership information.
American Guild of Musical Artists (AGMA)
1430 Broadway, 14th Floor
New York, NY 10018
Tel: 212-265-3687
http://www.musicalartists.org

For information on voluntary certifications, contact
American Guild of Organists
475 Riverside Drive, Suite 1260
New York, NY 10115
Tel: 212-870-2310
http://www.agohq.org

For information on the music summer camps program, contact
Interlochen Center for the Arts
PO Box 199
Interlochen, MI 49643

Tel: 231-276-7200
http://www.interlochen.org

This organization supports public outreach programs, promotes music education, and offers information on the career of music teacher.
MENC: The National Association for Music Education
1806 Robert Fulton Drive
Reston, VA 20191
Tel: 800-336-3768
http://www.menc.org

For information on membership, competitions for music students, and resources for music teachers, contact
Music Teachers National Association
441 Vine Street, Suite 505
Cincinnati, OH 45202
Tel: 888-512-5278
http://www.mtna.org

NASM is an organization of schools, colleges, and universities that provide music education. Visit the website for a listing of NASM-accredited institutions.
National Association of Schools of Music (NASM)
11250 Roger Bacon Drive, Suite 21
Reston, VA 20190
Tel: 703-437-0700
http://nasm.arts-accredit.org

This organization offers networking opportunities, career information, and a mentoring program for women in music.
Women In Music—National Network
31121 Mission Boulevard, Suite 300
Hayward, CA 94544
Tel: 510-232-3897
http://www.womeninmusic.com

Music Journalists

QUICK FACTS

School Subjects
Journalism
Music

Personal Skills
Artistic
Communication/ideas

Work Environment
Primarily indoors
Primarily multiple locations

Minimum Education Level
Bachelor's degree

Salary Range
$17,620 to $30,510 to
$69,450+

Certification or Licensing
None available

Outlook
About as fast as the average

DOT
131

GOE
11.08.02

NOC
5123

O*NET-SOC
27-3022.00

OVERVIEW

Music journalists report on the latest music releases and public performances of all genres. Their work appears in print and online newspapers and magazines, or is used in radio or television broadcasts. They work on periodical staffs or as freelance writers.

HISTORY

As newspapers have grown in size and widened the scope of their coverage, the number of employees and specialized jobs has increased. This includes assigning reporters to different *beats,* such as local and national news, sports, and entertainment. This latter category was soon subdivided into smaller groups, such as celebrity news, restaurant reviews, and music.

Today, the writings of music journalists are included in periodicals printed all over the country. These specialized reporters have become crucial parts of newspaper staffs and other news mediums, such as magazines, radio, and television. With the advent of the Internet, many periodicals are going online, bringing the work of many music journalists to the Web.

Most magazines and newspapers have sections that focus on entertainment; others, such as *Rolling Stone* and *Blender,* focus entirely on music reviews and reporting. In either case, music journalists will continue to be in demand to write knowledgeable and creative articles about artists, bands, record sales, and the music industry.

THE JOB

Music journalists write about new releases and recent performances of all types of musicians. They research artists or bands, watch or listen to them perform, and then write a review or story. Some music journalists also write columns for newspaper or magazine publication or commentary for radio or television broadcast.

Music journalists conduct their research by attending musical shows or listening to compact discs or music in other formats. If they are reviewing a live performance, they have to take notes of the concert's venue, crowd, atmosphere, and other factors that will make their review more interesting and thorough.

Though some music writers may simply report objectively on music news, most write criticism. To garner respect and credibility, their opinions on performances or recordings must be fair, but honest. To do this, music journalists compare the performance or album release with previous works of the artist or band in question and compare it with other similar music artists. For example, if a journalist is reviewing a young pop star's latest CD, he or she would not compare it to work of a classical orchestra, but perhaps might hold it up to work of rock stars from previous eras, such as the Beatles, Elvis Presley, or the Rolling Stones.

Music journalists write more than just reviews. They also write profiles of artists and bands. These stories may originate as an assignment from a music editor or as the result of a lead or news tip. Good music journalists are always on the lookout for new story ideas.

To write a personal music article, music journalists gather and verify facts by interviewing the artist or band and also talk to people involved in the production or organization of a music show or recording. During interviews, journalists generally take notes or use a tape recorder to collect information and write the story once back in their office. When under tight deadline, music journalists might have little time between their last interview and publication, and may enlist the help of editors and other writers to review and help organize their material. Together, they will decide what emphasis, or angle, to give the story and make sure it is written to meet prescribed standards of editorial style and format.

Music journalists are employed either as in-house staff or as freelance writers. Pay varies according to experience and the position, but freelancers must provide their own office space and equipment such as computers, phones, and fax machines. Freelance writers also are responsible for attracting clients, keeping tax records, sending out invoices, negotiating contracts, and providing their own health insurance.

REQUIREMENTS
High School
High school courses that will provide you with a firm foundation for a music reporting career include English, journalism, music history,

band, communications, typing, and computer science. Speech courses will help you hone your interviewing skills, which are necessary for success as a journalist. In addition, it will be helpful to take college prep courses, such as foreign language, history, math, and science.

Postsecondary Training

Most newspapers, magazines, and other employers of music journalists want reporters with at least a bachelor's degree, and a graduate degree will give you an advantage when applying for positions.

Many music writers have backgrounds in general journalism. More than 400 colleges offer bachelor's degrees in journalism. In these schools, approximately three-fourths of a student's time is devoted to a liberal arts education and one-fourth to the professional study of journalism, with required courses such as introductory mass media, basic reporting and copy editing, history of journalism, and press law and ethics. Students are encouraged to select other journalism courses according to their specific interests.

Other music journalists get their educational background in music. They may major in music theory, criticism, or performance and develop their writing skills by minoring in journalism or simply through reporting experience.

In addition to formal course work, most employers look for practical writing experience. If you have worked on high school or college newspapers, yearbooks, or literary magazines, you will make a better candidate, as well as if you have worked for small community newspapers or radio stations, even in unpaid positions. Many book publishers, magazines, newspapers, and radio and television stations have summer internship programs that provide valuable training if you want to learn about the publishing and broadcasting businesses. Interns do many simple tasks, such as running errands and answering phones, but some may be asked to perform research, conduct interviews, or even write some minor pieces.

Other Requirements

In order to succeed as a music journalist, you must have excellent typing and computer skills to write up stories under tight deadlines. Although not essential, knowledge of shorthand or speedwriting makes note taking easier, and an acquaintance with photography is an asset.

You must also be inquisitive, aggressive, persistent, and detail oriented. You should enjoy interaction with people of various races, cultures, religions, economic levels, and social statuses. For some jobs—on a newspaper, for example, where the activity is hectic and deadlines are short—the ability to concentrate and produce under pressure is essential.

Music criticism is a highly specialized field, one that blends music knowledge and expressive writing skills. The glamour of attending concerts and meeting musicians is an undeniable benefit. However, the journalist job also includes possible stress and irregular hours. To succeed as a journalist, you have to have passion about the subject in which you write. You should be able to appreciate all forms of music and have in-depth knowledge of the evolution of music trends, scenes, and sounds to place artists in their historical context.

EXPLORING

You can explore a career as a music journalist in a number of ways. Talk to reporters and editors at local newspapers and radio and TV stations. Interview the admissions counselor at the school of journalism closest to your home to get a sense of the type of students who apply and are accepted into journalism programs.

Think You Have What It Takes to Be a Critic?

A great way to explore the career of music journalist is to start thinking like one. Go to a music performance, whether it is a rock band or a symphony orchestra, and take mental or written notes about the performance. Then, after the show, write your own review. Ask the following questions:

- What was the venue like? Was your view of the artist or band obstructed in any way? How were the acoustics?

- Did other audience members seem interested in the show? Did the crowd participate in any manner?

- During the performance, did the song lyrics or sounds have a unifying theme?

- Were there dancers, accompanying singers, guest musicians, or other contributors to the show besides the main headliner? What did they contribute to the feel and quality of the performance?

- What was the overall experience of the performance? Would you recommend the show to a friend or family member?

You should also read the work of music journalists to get a sense of how they organize and structure their reviews and articles. Take note of when a music reporter writes a particularly positive or negative review and how he or she handles writing it honestly but tactfully. See the end of this article for websites of popular music magazines that publish excerpts of reviews online.

In addition to taking courses in English, journalism, music, speech, computer science, and typing, high school students can acquire practical experience by working on school newspapers or a community organization's newsletter. Part-time and summer jobs with newspapers or radio stations provide invaluable experience to the aspiring music reporter.

EMPLOYERS

Music journalists write for newspapers, magazines, wire services, and radio and television broadcasts. They may write for general news periodicals that have entertainment sections or for specialty music magazines, such as *Rolling Stone* or *Spin*. Some work as staff writers, but many are freelancers and write for several publications.

STARTING OUT

You need to acquire a fair amount of experience before you can call yourself a music journalist. Most people start out in entry-level positions, such as junior writer, copy editor, or researcher. These jobs may be listed with college placement offices or they can be obtained by applying directly to individual publishers or broadcasting companies. Graduates who previously held internships at newspapers, radio stations or related employers often have the advantage of knowing someone who can give them a personal recommendation and leads on jobs. Want ads in newspapers and trade journals are another source for jobs. Because of the competition for staff writer positions, however, few vacancies are listed with public or private employment agencies.

Once you schedule an interview, the employer will want to see samples of your published writing. These should be assembled in an organized portfolio or scrapbook. Bylined or signed articles are more credible (and, as a result, more useful) than stories from unidentified sources.

One helpful source when applying for jobs is the *Editor & Publisher International Year Book: The Encyclopedia of the Newspaper Industry* (New York, Editor & Publisher, 2003). This publication lists names and addresses of newspapers and other publishers and is available for reference in most public libraries.

ADVANCEMENT

Music journalists can advance in many ways. As they gain recognition and respect as music experts, they may be assigned to cover more highly anticipated concerts or music releases. They can also advance by working for larger newspapers, magazines, or other media outlets. They may choose to move into other reporting jobs, such as general entertainment reporter or editorial writer. Music journalists can also move into higher paying jobs such as head entertainment editor or even editor in chief of a music publication.

Freelance or self-employed writers earn advancement in the form of larger fees as they gain exposure and establish their reputations as music critics and writers.

EARNINGS

There are great variations in the earnings of music journalists. Salaries are related to experience, the type and size of media outlet for which the writer works, and geographic location.

According to the U.S. Department of Labor, the median salary for reporters was $30,510 in 2002. The lowest paid 10 percent of these workers earned $17,620 or less per year, while the highest paid 10 percent made $69,450 or more annually. In the same year, reporters who worked in radio and television broadcasting had average annual earnings of $46,260.

WORK ENVIRONMENT

Music journalists' jobs are sometimes glamorous, getting tickets to sold-out shows, hearing new albums before they are released to the public, or interviewing popular rock stars, bands, and other musicians. However, these reporters work under a great deal of pressure in settings that differ from the typical business office. Their physical surroundings range from private offices to noisy, crowded newsrooms filled with other workers typing and talking on the telephone. Music journalists also have to travel to music venues or studios to hear performances or conduct interviews. These work environments can be loud and/or dark—generally not the best settings in which to write.

Though the work can be hectic and stressful, music journalists are seldom bored. People who are the most content as music writers have a passion for music and enjoy and work well with deadline pressure.

OUTLOOK

The *Occupational Outlook Handbook* projects that the employment of reporters (in general) will grow more slowly than the average. However, specialty writers, such as music journalists, will more likely experience average employment growth due to their expertise and knowledge.

The demand for music journalists will be higher in large cities such as New York, Chicago, or Seattle because of their large and busy music scenes. But those just breaking into journalism might find better luck starting at smaller community newspapers and other publications. In general, opportunities will be best for writers who are willing to relocate and accept relatively low starting salaries. With experience, music writers at small papers can move up to editing positions or may choose to transfer to reporting jobs at larger newspapers or magazines.

A significant number of jobs will be provided by magazines and in radio and television broadcasting. For beginning music journalists, small stations with local news broadcasts will continue to replace staff who move on to larger stations or leave the business. Large network hiring has been cut drastically in the past few years and will probably continue to decline.

In addition, strong employment growth is expected for music journalists who write for online newspapers and magazines.

FOR MORE INFORMATION

This organization provides general educational information on all areas of journalism, including newspapers, magazines, television, and radio.
Association for Education in Journalism and Mass
    Communication
234 Outlet Pointe Boulevard
Columbia, SC 29210
Tel: 803-798-0271
http://www.aejmc.org

For information about careers in music, visit the following website:
MENC: The National Association for Music Education
1806 Robert Fulton Drive
Reston, VA 20191
Tel: 800-336-3768
http://www.menc.org

The following organization offers student memberships for those interested in opinion writing:
National Conference of Editorial Writers
3899 North Front Street
Harrisburg, PA 17110
Tel: 717-703-3015
http://www.ncew.org

Visit the following website to read music reviews and other news:
Association of Music Writers and Photographers
http://www.musicjournalist.com

Check out the following magazines' sites to read music reviews and profiles of current music artists:
Billboard
http://www.billboard.com

CMJ
http://www.cmj.com

Q
http://www.q4music.com

Rolling Stone
http://www.rollingstone.com

Music Librarians

QUICK FACTS

School Subjects
Computer science
Foreign language
Music

Personal Skills
Helping/teaching
Leadership/management

Work Environment
Primarily indoors
Primarily one location

Minimum Education Level
Master's degree

Salary Range
$24,510 to $43,090 to
$75,714+

Certification or Licensing
Required for certain positions

Outlook
About as fast as the average

DOT
100

GOE
11.02.04

NOC
5111

O*NET-SOC
25-4021.00

OVERVIEW

As prominent professionals in the information services field, *librarians* help others find information and select materials best suited to their needs. They are key personnel wherever books, magazines, audiovisual materials, and a variety of other informational materials are cataloged and kept. Librarians help make access to these reference materials possible. *Music librarians* perform many of the same duties as traditional librarians, but specialize in managing materials related to music. Approximately 149,000 librarians are employed in positions throughout the country. Music librarians make up a small percentage of this number.

HISTORY

The oldest known musical notation appears on a Mesopotamian cuneiform tablet from about 1800 B.C. Such inscriptions were probably organized and arranged in libraries that were available only to members of royalty, very wealthy people, or religious groups that devoted time and effort to transcription. The people who were charged with caring for collections within these libraries could be considered the world's first music librarians.

Libraries continued to be available only to the elite until the Middle Ages, when many private institutions were destroyed by wars. The preservation of many ancient library materials can be attributed to orders of monks who diligently copied ancient Greek and Roman texts, as well as the Bible and other religious texts, and protected materials in their monasteries. The invention of the printing press in the 15th century allowed books and other printed material to be made more quickly and disseminated more widely. Books went from palaces and churches to the homes of the common people.

In the United States, the first music library was established by the Brooklyn (New York) Public Library in 1882. The Library of Congress Division of Music was organized in the 1890s, with a phonorecord collection established at the institution in 1903. By the early 20th century, music-related resources gained popular appeal in our nation's libraries. In fact, *Library Journal* devoted its August 1915 issue to the music collections of public libraries. By 1928, 53 colleges and universities had libraries with music collections—although only 12 of these collections featured audio recordings. In 1931, the Music Library Association (MLA) was formed to represent the professional interests of music librarians. Today's music librarians not only manage and organize music manuscripts, books, and recordings, but also must have a keen knowledge of the Internet and music computer software programs.

THE JOB

Music librarians perform many of the same tasks as general librarians. These duties, with an emphasis on music, include arranging, cataloging, and maintaining library collections; helping patrons find materials and advising them on how to use resources effectively; creating catalogs, indexes, brochures, exhibits, websites, and bibliographies to educate users about the library's resources; supervising the purchase and maintenance of the equipment needed to use these materials; hiring, training, and supervising library staff; setting and implementing budgets; and keeping abreast of developments in the field. They also select and acquire music, videotapes, records, cassettes, DVDs, compact discs, books, manuscripts, and other nonbook materials for the library; this entails evaluating newly published materials as well as seeking out older materials.

Specialized duties for music librarians vary based on their employer and their skill set. For example, a music librarian employed by a college, university, or conservatory may acquire the music needed by student musical groups, while a librarian who is employed by music publishers may help edit musical publications. Music librarians employed by radio and television stations catalog and oversee music-related materials that are used solely by employees of these organizations. They research and recommend music selections for programs, pull and refile musical selections for on-air shifts, and maintain relationships with record companies and distributors.

Some music librarians may arrange special music-related courses, presentations, or performances at their libraries. They may also compile lists of books, periodicals, articles, and audiovisual materials on music, or they may teach others how to do this.

Music librarians at large libraries may specialize in one particular task. *Music catalogers* are librarians who specialize in the cataloging and classification of music-related materials such as scores and sound recordings, software, audiovisual materials, and books. *Music bibliographers* create detailed lists of music-related materials for use by library patrons. These lists may be organized by subject, language, date, composer, musician, or other criteria.

In addition to their regular duties, some music librarians teach music- or library science-related courses at colleges and universities. Others write reviews of books and music for print and online publications.

REQUIREMENTS

High School

If you are interested in becoming a music librarian, be sure to take a full college preparatory course load. Focus on classes in music, English, speech, history, and foreign languages. Learning how to use a computer and conduct basic research in a library is essential. Developing these skills will not only aid in your future library work, but will also help you in college and in any other career areas you decide to pursue.

Postsecondary Training

Most students interested in becoming music librarians pursue undergraduate education in a music-related field. In the late 1990s, the MLA surveyed its members regarding educational achievement. The majority of its members who received a bachelor's degree in the arts or music majored in the following subjects: musicology, music education, music theory/composition, and vocal and instrumental performance.

In addition to music-related courses, be sure to study at least one foreign language since music and music literature are published in many languages. The MLA reports that the most popular foreign languages (in descending order) of its members were German, French, Italian, Spanish, Latin, and Russian. You should also take classes that strengthen your communication skills, research methods, collection organization, and customer service skills. More than half of the accredited library schools do not require students to take introductory courses in library science while an undergraduate. It would be wise, though, to check with schools for specific requirements.

You will need to earn a master's degree to become a librarian. The degree is generally known as the master of library science (M.L.S), but in some institutions it may be referred to by a different title, such as the master of library and information science. You should plan to attend a graduate school of library and information science that is accredited by the American Library Association (ALA). Currently, there are more than 56 ALA-accredited graduate schools. Some libraries will not consider job applicants who attended a nonaccredited school.

A second master's degree in music is usually required for the best music librarianship positions. Some schools offer a dual degree in librarianship and music. Common combinations include an M.L.S. with either a master of arts in musicology, a master of music in music history, or a master of music in music theory. Other schools may allow students to take music courses that can be counted toward a library degree. Typical graduate courses include music librarianship, music bibliography, music cataloging, music libraries and information services, history of music printing, history of music documents, and special problems in music cataloging. Other graduate courses may feature sections that relate to music librarianship. Many graduate programs also offer internships or practicums in which students can gain hands-on experience working in a music library.

The *Directory of Library School Offerings in Musical Librarianship,* published by the Music Library Association, provides information on U.S. and Canadian library schools that offer a master's degree in library science with a concentration in music, specialized courses in music librarianship, or other music-related educational opportunities. A free, online version of the publication is available at the MLA website (http://www.musiclibraryassoc.org); a print version may be ordered from the association for a small fee.

A doctorate may be required for work in research libraries, university libraries, or special collections. A doctorate is commonly required for the top administrative posts of these types of libraries, as well as for faculty positions in graduate schools of library science.

Certification or Licensing

There is no specialized certification available for music librarians. If you plan to work outside of music librarianship as a school librarian, you are required to earn teacher's certification in addition to preparation as a librarian. You may also be required to earn a master's degree in education. Various state, county, and local governments have set up other requirements for education and certification. Contact the school board in the area in which you are interested in working for specific requirements. Your public library system should also have information readily available.

The ALA is currently developing a voluntary certification program to recognize individuals who have demonstrated knowledge and skills in general library science and to promote professional development.

Other Requirements

Music librarians should have an excellent memory and a keen eye for detail, as they manage a wide variety of resources. They must love music and be willing to assist others with sometimes obscure or demanding requests.

Music librarians who deal with the public should have strong interpersonal skills, tact, and patience. An imaginative, highly motivated, and resourceful personality is very valuable. An affinity for problem solving is another desirable quality. Librarians are often expected to take part in community affairs, cooperating in the preparation of exhibits, presenting book reviews, and explaining library use to community organizations. As a music librarian, you will also need to be a leader in developing the cultural and musical tastes of library patrons.

Music librarians involved with technical services should be detail-oriented, have good planning skills, and be able to think analytically. They should have a love for information and be willing to master the techniques for obtaining and presenting knowledge. Librarians must also be prepared to master constantly changing technology.

EXPLORING

There are several ways you can explore the field of music librarianship and librarianship in general. If you are a high school student, you already have your own personal experiences with the library: reading, doing research for class projects, or just browsing. If this experience sparks an interest in library work, you can talk with a school or community librarian whose own experiences in the field can provide a good idea of what goes on behind the scenes. Some schools may have library clubs you can join to learn about library work. If one doesn't exist, you could consider starting your own library club.

You should also try to take as many music-related classes as possible in high school. These will begin to give you the basic framework you need to become a music librarian. Ask your school librarian to

Books about Music Librarianship

Abromeit, Kathleen, Gregg Geary, and Laura Snyder. *Music Library Instruction*. Lanham, Md.: Scarecrow Press, 2004.

Blair, Linda and Paula Elliot, eds. *Careers in Music Librarianship II: Traditions and Transitions*. Lanham, Md.: Scarecrow Press, 2004.

Bradley, Carol June. *American Librarianship: A Biographical and Historical Survey*. Westport, Conn.: Greenwood Publishing Group, 1990.

Carli, Alice. *Binding and Care of Printed Music*. Lanham, Md.: Scarecrow Press, 2003.

Mann, Alfred, ed. *Modern Music Librarianship: Essays in Honor of Ruth Watanabe*. Hillsdale, N.Y.: Pendragon Press, 1989.

McKnight, Mark. *Music Classification Systems*. Lanham, Md.: Scarecrow Press, 2002.

Tatian, Carol. *Careers in Music Librarianship: Perspectives from the Field*. Lanham, Md.: Scarecrow Press, 1991.

direct you to books and other resources about music. You can also ask him or her to help you learn more about music librarian careers.

Once you know you are interested in library work, you might be able to work as an assistant in the school library media center or find part-time work in a local public library. Such volunteer or paid positions may provide you with experience checking materials in and out at the circulation desk, shelving returned books, or typing title, subject, and author information on cards or in computer records. In college, you might be able to work as a technical or clerical assistant in your school's music library.

Contact the MLA or the ALA to inquire about student memberships. Many library associations offer excellent mentoring opportunities as well. Finally, if you have an email account, sign up for one or more of the listservs offered by these groups. A listserv is an email list of professionals throughout the world who consult each other on special topics. By subscribing to a listserv, you can discover what matters concern professional librarians today. Before you post your own comment or query, however, be sure you know the rules and regulations created by the list's moderator, and always be respectful of others.

EMPLOYERS

Music librarians are employed at large research libraries such as the Library of Congress; colleges, universities, and conservatories; public and private libraries; archives; radio and television stations; and musical societies and foundations. They also work for professional bands and orchestras, music publishing companies, and the military.

As the field of library and information services grows, music librarians can find more work outside the traditional library setting. Experienced music librarians may advise libraries or other agencies on information systems, library renovation projects, or other information-based issues.

STARTING OUT

Generally, music librarians must complete all educational requirements before applying for a job. In some cases, part-time work experience or completing an internship while in graduate school may lead to a full-time position upon graduation. Some employers may even allow an especially promising applicant to begin learning on the job before the library degree is conferred.

Upon graduating, new music librarians should consult the placement offices at their school. Employers seeking new graduates often recruit through library schools. Most professional library and information science organizations have job listings that candidates can consult. For example, the MLA offers a Joblist at its website. Music librarians can also use online job search engines to help locate an appropriate position. Newspaper classifieds may be of some help in locating a job, although other approaches may be more appropriate to this profession.

Many music librarians entering the workforce today are combining their experience in another career with graduate library and information science education. For example, a music teacher who plays trumpet in a band could mix her part-time teaching experience and her hobby with a degree in library science to begin a full-time career as a music librarian. Almost any music-related background can be used to advantage when entering the field of musical librarianship.

Individuals interested in working in musical library positions for the federal government can contact the human resources department—or consult the website—of the government agency for which they are interested in working; for these government positions, applicants must take a civil service examination. Public libraries, too, often follow a civil service system of appointment.

ADVANCEMENT

The beginning music librarian may gain experience by taking a job as an assistant. He or she can learn a lot from practical experience before attempting to manage a department or entire library. A music librarian may advance to positions with greater levels of responsibility within the same library system, or he or she may gain initial experience in a small library and then advance by transferring to a larger or more specialized library. Within a large library, promotions to higher positions are possible (for example, to the supervision of a department). Experienced music librarians with the necessary qualifications may advance to positions in library administration, such as *library director,* who is at the head of a typical library organizational scheme. This professional sets library policies and plans and administers programs of library services, usually under the guidance of a governing body, such as a board of directors or board of trustees. Library directors have overall responsibility for the operation of a library system. A doctorate is desirable for reaching top administrative levels, as well as for landing a graduate library school faculty position.

Experienced music librarians, in particular those with strong administrative, computer, or planning backgrounds, may move into the area of information consulting. They use their expertise to advise libraries and other organizations on issues regarding information services. Other experienced librarians, especially those with computer experience, may also go into specialized areas of library work, becoming increasingly valuable to business and industry, as well as other fields.

EARNINGS

Salaries for music librarians depend on such factors as the location, size, and type of library, the amount of experience the librarian has, and the responsibilities of the position. According to the U.S. Department of Labor, median annual earnings of all librarians in 2002 were $43,090. Salaries ranged from less than $24,510 to more than $66,590. Librarians working in colleges and universities earned $43,050. Librarians employed in local government earned $38,370 in 2000. In the federal government, the average salary for all librarians was $63,651 in 2001.

The American Library Association's Survey of Librarian Salaries reports the following mean salaries for librarians and managers in 2002: library directors, $75,714; deputy/associate/assistant directors,

$62,847; managers/supervisors of support staff, $44,549; librarians who do not supervise, $44,279; and beginning librarians, $35,051.

Most music librarians receive a full benefits package, which may include paid vacation time, holiday pay, compensated sick leave, various insurance plans, and retirement savings programs. Librarians who work in a college or university library may receive tuition waivers to help them earn advanced degrees in their field.

WORK ENVIRONMENT

Most libraries are pleasant and comfortable places in which to assist those doing research, studying, or reading or listening for pleasure. Music librarians must constantly read about and listen to music to keep informed in order to serve library patrons. They must also strive to stay abreast of constantly changing technology, which may seem overwhelming at times.

Some music librarians may find the work demanding and stressful when they deal with users who are working under deadline pressure. Librarians working as music catalogers may suffer eyestrain and headaches from working long hours at a computer screen.

On the average, librarians work between 35 and 40 hours per week. Since most libraries are open evenings and weekends to accommodate the schedules of their users, many librarians will have a nontraditional work schedule, working, for instance, from 11:00 A.M. to 9:00 P.M., or taking Monday and Tuesday as a weekend in lieu of Saturday and Sunday.

There is, of course, some routine in library work, but the trend is to place clerical duties in the hands of library technicians and library assistants, freeing the professional music librarian for administrative, research, personnel, and community services. For the most part, music librarians tend to find the work intellectually stimulating, challenging, and dynamic. The knowledge that one is providing so many valuable services to the community and one's employer can be extremely rewarding.

OUTLOOK

The American Library Association (ALA) predicts a serious shortage of librarians in the next five to 12 years. The Association reports that one in four librarians is expected to retire in the next five to seven years, and approximately half will retire within 12 years. Thus, opportunities for librarians in general should be good.

Employment prospects for music librarians will not be as strong. The field of musical librarianship is small, and there is little turnover in the best positions. Music librarians with advanced education and knowledge of more than one foreign language will have the best employment prospects. Employment opportunities will also arise for music librarians who have a background in information science and library automation. The rapidly expanding field of information management has created a demand for qualified people to set up and maintain information systems for private industry and consulting firms.

FOR MORE INFORMATION

For information on careers, accredited graduate schools of library and information science, scholarships and grants, and college student membership, contact
American Library Association
50 East Huron Street
Chicago, IL 60611
Tel: 800-545-2433
Email: membership@ala.org
http://www.ala.org

For a list of graduate programs in musicology, contact
American Musicological Society
201 South 34th Street
Philadelphia, PA 19104
Tel: 215-898-8698
http://www.sas.upenn.edu/music/ams
or http://www.theams.us

For information on careers, educational options in music librarianship, and student membership, contact
Music Library Association
8551 Research Way, Suite 180
Middleton, WI 53562
Tel: 608-836-5825
http://www.musiclibraryassoc.org

For a wide variety of music librarianship resources, visit
Music Library Association Clearinghouse
http://www.music.indiana.edu/tech_s/mla

This website features descriptions of and links to ethnomusicology degree programs.

    Society for Ethnomusicology
    1165 East 3rd Street
    Morrison Hall 005
    Indiana University
    Bloomington, IN 47405
    Tel: (812) 855-6673
    http://www.ethnomusicology.org

For information on working in a specialized library, contact
    Special Libraries Association
    1700 18th Street, NW
    Washington, DC 20009
    Tel: 202-234-4700
    http://www.sla.org

For information on librarianship in Canada, contact
    Canadian Library Association
    328 Frank Street
    Ottawa, ON K2P 0X8 Canada
    Tel: 613-232-9625
    http://www.cla.ca

Music Producers

OVERVIEW

Music producers are responsible for the overall production of commercially recorded music. They work closely with recording artists and audio recording engineers to ensure everything runs smoothly and according to plan during a recording session. They monitor and control the technical aspects of a session, such as microphone placement, tracks used, sound and effects, musician needs, and anything else that influences the quality of the recorded music, and they see to other needs of the musicians and recording engineers. They review prospective new artists, maintain ties with contracted artists, and may negotiate contract and recording arrangements. They also work on the final mixing and editing of the recording.

HISTORY

By the 1950s, producers were the key people in the record industry. They sought the talent to make hit recordings and often picked the material to be recorded. Until the mid-1950s producers were generally producing seven-inch, single records, often hiring arrangers to write the musical arrangement. In the mid-1950s, with the beginning of rock and roll, emphasis switched to full-length 12-inch records with multiple songs from the same artist. In the late 1950s, a relatively new factor appeared in the music business: the independent music producer. Until this time producers worked mostly for the record companies. The independents, however, hired their talents out to the studios by claiming they had the connections and vision to produce the next hit. They took over all elements necessary to produce the recording. Soon producers began to make their own contracts with the artists, produce the records independently, and then sell them to the record companies for distribution.

The producer's job description remained pretty much the same until the early 1980s, when the music videos became an important part of a record's success. Music videos drastically changed the rules some producers lived by. Now they not only had to worry about hiring talent, audio recording engineers, and sound technicians, but also set and costume designers, video technicians, film directors, choreographers, and other skilled workers who worked for visual effects. They had to learn the basics of film production in order to help direct video production, just as they do for recording. Today there are some producers that work exclusively with video.

THE JOB

Artistry and experimentation aside, the goal of the successful music producer is to produce profit-making recordings that sound as good as they possibly can.

Fran Allen-Leake works as a music producer; she's also a promotion specialist and does A&R (artist and repertoire) work and some artist management. "I'm a jack of all trades in the music industry," she says. She is also on the board of governors for the Chicago chapter of the National Academy of Recording Arts & Sciences, the organization that presents the Grammy Awards. "The producer's job is to paint the musical picture," she says. This involves determining the tunes that will go on the artist's CD and putting together the music team.

Music producers have to be creative and innovative, with their own style and method for achieving set goals. The degree of involvement a producer has with a recording project varies from producer to producer: some are involved in every phase of production, and some (those at major labels) handle only certain elements and assign the rest to specialists. Most producers, however, will at least put together the talent (if it is not already there in the form of an established band or orchestra) and the music that will make a recording. Some producers, particularly the independents, arrange for the recording studio, technicians, and background musicians, and they frequently become involved in the mixing and editing of a recording, album cover art, packaging, contracts, administrative paperwork, and marketing and promotion. In a major record company some of these elements are more likely to be handled by separate departments.

Music producers usually specialize in a certain musical genre, be it rock and roll, rap, country and western, jazz, or classical. A record company may specialize in all, several, or one of the musical genres.

Unlike many producers who specialize, Allen-Leake has worked in a variety of musical genres. "I've worked on everything from rock to R&B and blues," she says. "As a producer, you have to have an appreciation of the musical format. You have to know all music genres and be able to anticipate what's going to happen in the industry."

Music producers never stop seeking new talent or projects to record. They keep close contact with the label A&R staff, whose job it is to scout up-and-coming talent, or they find talent on their own. Some producers build talent by assembling a group of musicians to release a recording or series of recordings that the producer feels will be successful based on the musicians' skill and reputation.

Producers discover new talent in a number of ways. Personal contacts are one of the most important methods; managers, musicians, conductors, songwriters, and arrangers often introduce the producer to a band or solo artist. Musicians frequently send demo tapes to record labels and producers they feel might take an interest in their music. Many producers find talent on independent labels. Since the success of the one-time independent label rock band Nirvana in early 1990s, there has been an influx of so-called *indie* bands (indie is industry slang for independent) signing on to the major labels. Other leads may come through reading the show business trade papers, such as *Variety* and *Billboard*. Once the producer finds up-and-coming talent, he or she offers contractual negotiations to the musicians, which may involve the musicians' agents or managers and lawyers.

After the talent has been signed, the producer usually will have to prepare a budget covering all of the expenses of production. The next step might be setting up a rehearsal schedule and making arrangements for a rehearsal studio. Depending on the project, the producer either selects the songs the talent will record, or he or she lets the musicians decide and make suggestions on ways to make the songs fit better in the label's target market.

After consulting with the musicians, the producer selects the recording studio and the audio recording engineers who will control the quality of the recording. Producers make sure that all necessary equipment and instruments are available at the studio during the scheduled sessions. Some record companies have their own recording studios, which are convenient and save costs. Independent producers can be more flexible in their choice of studios and often choose places other than studios to record. Because some major recordings may take months and hundreds of hours in the studio, producers make sure the atmosphere is comfortable for the musicians. Most producers work closely with the recording engineers to get the most desirable sound quality during the session. They frequently adjust levels, microphone placement, sound quality, and other factors to improve the recording.

After the recording session, time allowing, producers wait a short period of time—a few days or a week or more—before attempting the final editing of the multitrack recording into a two-track stereo master. This process is called the mix. Mixing involves determining in which part of the stereo sound spectrum each recorded track will be placed to produce the optimal effect. This can be an enormously complex process, especially when some recordings have more than 24 tracks. During the mixing process other musical elements can be added, such as instrumental or vocal background, echo, and other sound effects. Mixing can go on for days even though the process has been sped up through the use of computerized mixing boards.

After the producer is satisfied with the mix, a master is made from which CDs, tapes, and (occasionally) records can be manufactured. The producer also may oversee the mastering to be sure of the final quality of the recording before manufacturing begins. "I like to look at the mastering as the 'smoothing over,'" Allen-Leake says. "A bad mastering job can screw up all the work you've done on the mix. Ideally, I'm looking for enhancement." After the manufacturing process, the recording is ready for distribution and promotion. Radio stations and reviewers are given promotional copies of the recording. Personal appearances on television and radio talk shows are booked for the talent where possible, and a tour is scheduled to support the new release. From a rock, rap, or country recording session, producers and label executives decide which song will be the likely hit, and from this song, a video is made, which is just as important and complex as the recording itself.

REQUIREMENTS

High School

Begin your musical training as early as possible. Take courses in music and band to learn something about instruments, voice, and music theory. Learn about as many music genres as you can, including classical and jazz. Music is often affected by social issues, so courses in journalism, government, and history provide useful background knowledge. Classes in media, broadcast journalism, and theater may involve you with sound engineering.

Postsecondary Training

After high school, you should seek postsecondary training in audio engineering. To learn about educational opportunities in the United

The Benefits of Music Education

According to information gathered by MENC: The National Association for Music Education, music has the following far-reaching effects on students:

- Secondary school students who were members of an orchestra or band reported the lowest usage of alcohol, tobacco, and illegal drugs. (Source: Texas Commission on Drug and Alcohol Abuse Report, January, 1998)

- Students with coursework or experience in musical performance and music appreciation had higher SAT scores than did students with no musical experience. (Source: The College Board)

- Researchers have determined that children who take piano lessons have improved spatial-temporal IQ scores; spatial-temporal thinking plays a role in some types of mathematical reasoning. (Source: Neurological Research)

States and abroad, visit the websites of the Audio Engineering Society (http://www.aes.org) or *Mix* online (http://mixonline.com).

The most basic level of education is attending seminars and workshops. This may be the best way to obtain an early, hands-on understanding of music recording. These programs are generally intended to introduce new technologies in the audio field. A seminar can last a few hours or several weeks. Many workshops are geared toward introducing a certain aspect of recording, such as mixing, editing, or music production. Workshops can prepare you for entry-level apprenticeships at a recording studio.

If you are looking for a more comprehensive course of study in specific areas of the recording industry, you can enroll in a trade school program. Depending on the curriculum, these programs can take from several weeks to up to a year to complete. The most complete level of postsecondary education is a two- or four-year degree from a university. At a university, you will find an ideal learning environment complete with state-of-the-art equipment and a teaching staff of knowledgeable professionals. Universities incorporate music, music technology, and music business in a comprehensive curriculum that prepares their graduates to be highly competitive in the industry. At a university students can enroll in other nonaudio courses necessary for the successful producer, such as courses in business, communications, public relations, and computers.

Other Requirements

"Producing takes a lot of understanding of how people work," Fran Allen-Leake says. "You need an understanding of artists." To get this understanding, she spent a few years working as a vocalist, "so I could really understand what it's like to be on the other side of the microphone."

Music producers must also have the instincts of artists to help artists record the best work they can. You should have a good ear for the music as well as a great deal of insight into the history and current trends of the recording industry.

EXPLORING

Join a music group to get a sense of the collaborative process of putting songs together. Your school may have equipment available for recording performances—your school's music teacher or media department director may be able to assist you in a recording project. Since a large part of being a producer involves good communication skills, any experience you can get dealing with a variety of people— as in a retail sales job, for example—will be helpful.

"Listen to everything," Fran Allen-Leake advises. "When listening, try to get a sense of the picture. What is the artist and producer trying to get across? What do they want you to feel? Read the back of every CD, and start getting familiar with the names of producers. You'll see some of the names over and over again."

Students can contact record companies or recording studios to get more information; local studios can usually be found in the classified telephone directory, and others can be located in the music trade papers. The National Academy of Recording Arts & Sciences can provide information on the industry, or it can suggest where such information is available. There are also numerous books and music trade magazines that cover music production.

EMPLOYERS

Music producers work independently (freelance) or for a record company (usually referred to as a label). When working independently, they may be hired by a label for a project or they may bring their own artists to the attention of industry executives. Although many producers work in major cities such as New York, Chicago, and Los Angeles, many cities across the country have vibrant music scenes. Wherever there are recording studios and musicians, there will be a need for producers.

STARTING OUT

Postsecondary training in audio and recording technology will provide a strong basis for getting a job in music production, or at least in the music industry. Most training programs offer job placement assistance for their graduates, and record labels that are looking for producers frequently post job openings at schools that offer such programs. Some of the larger record labels offer highly competitive and much sought after internships in music recording. Students who finish an internship for a major record label will have a high success rate in finding employment. A job in any capacity with a record label, an independent producer, or in a recording studio would be worthwhile just to get your foot in the door. Many major labels prefer to hire only producers who have first worked independently.

To find a job as a music producer you have to be aggressive in canvassing the record companies and related businesses by telephone and mail to seek out entry-level jobs. Leads to jobs in the industry can also come through studying trade publications. These include *Billboard* (http://www.billboard.com), *Variety* (http://www.variety.com), *EQ* (http://www.eqmag.com), *Radio & Records* (http://www.rronline.com), *Mix* (http://www.mixonline.com), and *Down Beat* (http://www.downbeat.com).

ADVANCEMENT

Music producers advance as they continually produce projects that are successful commercially or, at the very least, in the eyes of the musicians and record label. There is no limit to where a successful music producer may go. Music producers already have a high degree of responsibility with a record label, as their work is directly reflected in the sales and profits of a recording. Producers who consistently produce profitable hits will be in high demand and will have the luxury of choosing labels and artists. Independent producers are already their own bosses, but if they are exceptionally good, record companies may want to put them under contract. Similarly, producers with record companies may see a brighter future as independent producers.

Within a major record label, producers could become heads of any of several departments, but they are most directly in line for the directorship or vice presidency of the A&R department. Depending on their talents and career goals, producers might also move into sales, publicity and public relations, advertising, marketing, or promotion. Some producers, whose sound or style is particularly sought after, may go on to start their own recording studios.

EARNINGS

A music producer can earn a considerable amount of money or go broke. It is difficult to indicate an average salary for producers because they generally make a lot of money or their tenure in the business is short. This is because the income of a record producer is directly tied to the sales of the records he or she produces. An independent producer works on a royalty basis, which usually is about 3–5 percent (also called points) of retail sales. They may also charge a fee or get an advance from the record company, which would be deducted from sales.

Starting out, producers often work as technicians for studios, making $18,540 or less a year in 2002, according to the U.S. Department of Labor (USDL). The USDL reports that the median salary for audio and video equipment technicians was $31,110 in 2002, and the median salary for sound engineering technicians was $36,970. The median salary for producers and directors (including those who work in film, theater, and broadcasting) was $46,240 in 2002, and salaries ranged from less than $23,300 to $119,760. Producers who work with leading performers in the industry can earn well over $200,000 a year.

Benefits packages vary from business to business. Music producers employed by a recording company can expect health insurance and paid vacation. Other benefits may include dental and eye care, life and disability insurance, and a pension plan. A producer's salary can increase by yearly bonuses or profit sharing if the company does well in the course of a year.

WORK ENVIRONMENT

Music producers have the opportunity to work closely with creative people. They also have an actual CD as a finished product. "There's a great deal of pride in authorship," Fran Allen-Leake says. But to stay competitive and in demand, producers must work very hard, sometimes weeks on end without a break. "The hours are unbelievably crazy," she says. The traveling can also be demanding. "Generally, every month I'm gone for some period of time. Could be five days, or three days, or three weeks."

A music producer at a record company usually has a private office and all of the support staff he or she needs. Recording studio space is supplied by the company and is either under its own ownership or contracted as necessary. Staff producers have expense accounts that are fairly unlimited so that they can entertain and travel when necessary. Independent producers may have situations similar to that of staff producers, or they may work out of their homes or apartments and rent space as needed.

A producer working steadily is frequently under a lot of pressure, especially during rehearsals and recording sessions, when high-priced talent is tied up and the producer must produce dramatic results within a limited amount of time.

OUTLOOK

The recording industry is in a continual state of flux. New technology, new music, new markets, and new ways of doing business are constantly redefining the way music producers perform their jobs. Computer technology is simplifying the recording and mixing process while opening new outlets for creativity. Employment for music producers is very competitive. Although some independent-label bands choose to produce themselves, the experience and know-how of a successful producer is a standard for major-label productions. Record labels will continue to seek the specialized skills of the music producer.

Thousands of recording companies exist in the United States, and their receipts measure in the billions of dollars. Every time a new technology is developed or any time a new musical trend develops, especially in the pop field, it gives the industry as well as the music producer a lift. Although the recording industry has undergone considerable consolidation in recent years (five mega-companies control 80 percent of the industry), music producers with an eye for talent and technical acumen will continue to enjoy good employment prospects in the industry.

FOR MORE INFORMATION

Visit the NARAS website to read about efforts to support the recording industry and to check out links to many music and recording-related sites.

National Academy of Recording Arts & Sciences (NARAS)
3402 Pico Boulevard
Santa Monica, CA 90405
Tel: 310-392-3777
http://grammy.com

For facts and statistics about the recording industry, contact
Recording Industry Association of America
1330 Connecticut Avenue, NW, Suite 300
Washington, DC 20036
Tel: 202-775-0101
http://www.riaa.com

For information on membership, contact
Society of Professional Audio Recording Services
PO Box 770845
Memphis, TN 38117
Tel: 800-771-7727
http://www.spars.com

Music Teachers

OVERVIEW

Music teachers instruct people on how to sing, play musical instruments, and appreciate and enjoy the world of music. They teach private lessons and classes. They may work at home or in a studio, school, college, or conservatory. Many music teachers are also performing musicians.

HISTORY

Music has been part of social and religious culture since the dawn of civilization. In music—as well as in politics, philosophy, and science—Western civilization has been influenced by the Greeks. The very word *music* has Greek roots, although it should be noted that what the Greeks called music included all of what are now called the liberal arts. In the West, music was also strongly influenced by the Roman Catholic Church. In fact, in the medieval period, the only places where formal musical education could be found were the Church's song schools, which trained boys to sing in religious services. The music that those boys sang was called plainsong, plainchant, or Gregorian chant. During this era and through the time of the Reformation, music was taught at monasteries and religious schools. Out of these schools grew the first universities that taught students both *musica speculative* (music theory) and *musica practica* (applied music). During this time, music education was also introduced in German and Italian schools.

In the United States, music education made gradual advances when cultural anchors such as churches and schools were established. In

QUICK FACTS

School Subjects
Music
Speech

Personal Skills
Communication/ideas
Helping/teaching

Work Environment
Primarily indoors
One location with some
travel

Minimum Education Level
Bachelor's degree

Salary Range
$19,000 to $47,560 to
$85,620+

Certification or Licensing
Voluntary (certification)
Required for certain positions (licensing)

Outlook
About as fast as the average

DOT
152

GOE
01.04.01

NOC
4131, 4141, 4142, 5133

O*NET-SOC
25-1121.00

1833, Lowell Mason, a church music director and bank teller, founded the Boston Academy of Music. He is largely considered to be the first music teacher in an American public school. In 1838, the Boston School Committee accepted music as a school subject. In the decades that followed, music became an accepted curricular subject in schools at all grade levels. The Music Teachers National Association, a professional, nonprofit organization of music teachers, was founded in 1876. It was the first professional association of its kind for music teachers in the United States. More than 30 years later, the Music Educators National Conference was founded. Today, its membership includes music teachers, university faculty and researchers, high school honor society members, and college students preparing to be music teachers. (The association changed its name in 1998 to MENC: The National Association for Music Education to better reflect its mission.)

In the early 1900s, Dr. Frank Damrosch, the head of music education for New York City's public schools, had the idea of establishing an American musical academy that would rival the music schools in Europe. In 1905, he formed the Juilliard School (then known as the Institute of Musical Art) as the first step toward bringing quality music education to the United States. Music education at all levels flourished for most of the 20th century. However, by the 1970s and 1980s, public school districts began to cut music education programs in an effort to save money and create funding for the introduction of computer science and other new classes.

In response to these budget cuts, music educators began to push for the reinstatement of arts-based programs in schools, citing studies that show that the benefits of art and music education for students carry over to other subjects and in everyday life. In 1983, *Nation at Risk,* a report about the educational deficiencies of U.S. students, was published by the U.S. Department of Education's National Commission on Excellence in Education, sparking a renewed interest in and emphasis on educational subjects that included the arts.

In the early 1990s, The Consortium of National Arts Education Associations developed the National Standards for Arts Education, which detailed what a strong education in the arts (music, dance, theater, and the visual arts) should provide. The passage of the Goals 2000: Educate America Act by Congress acknowledged, according to MENC, that the "arts are a core subject, as important to education as English, mathematics, history, civics and government, geography, science, and foreign language." Today, music education programs are growing again in popularity at all academic levels.

THE JOB

Music teachers help students learn to read music, develop their voices, breathe correctly, and hold and play their instruments properly. As their students master the techniques of their art, teachers guide them through more and more difficult pieces of music. Music teachers often organize recitals or concerts that feature their students. These recitals allow family and friends to hear how the students are progressing and help students get performing experience.

Elementary school music teachers teach basic music concepts and simple instruments to students, gradually adding more advanced topics or instrument instruction. They teach introductory lessons in music reading, music appreciation, and vocal and instrumental music. They may organize musical programs for pageants, plays, and other school events.

Secondary school music teachers teach music history, music appreciation, music theory, and other music-related courses to students in group and/or one-on-one lessons. They also teach students how to play percussion, wind, and string instruments. They direct in-school glee clubs, concert choirs, choral groups, marching bands, or orchestras. Since music is usually an elective at the high school level, music teachers often work with students who have some musical knowledge or ability.

College and university music teachers are also frequently performers or composers. They divide their time between group and individual instruction and may teach several music subjects, such as music appreciation and music history, arrangement, composition, conducting, theory, and pedagogy (the teaching of music). They use lectures, quizzes and tests, listening exercises in a musical laboratory, and performance before a jury (a group of faculty music teachers) to educate and assess the abilities of their students.

Private music teachers, also known as *studio music teachers,* may teach children who are just beginning to play or sing, teens who hope to make music their career, or adults who are interested in music lessons for their own enjoyment. They teach these students in a studio, in their homes, or at their students' homes. Private music teachers who teach music to very young children are sometimes known as *early childhood music educators.*

In addition to teaching students, music teachers also perform administrative tasks, such as assessing and grading the performance of their students, keeping attendance records, ordering supplies, storing and maintaining musical instruments and other classroom materials, and meeting with parents to discuss the performance of their

Music teachers need excellent communication skills in order to be able to work with students of all ages. *(Photo Disc)*

children. They also plan classroom lessons based on local or state requirements and the National Standards for Music Education.

To earn extra income, music teachers may also direct school musicals or community choirs or other musical groups, work in community theater, or perform as musicians or singers. Some music teachers also work as freelance music writers, composers and arrangers, and in other music-related professions.

REQUIREMENTS

High School
If you are interested in becoming a music teacher, you should take voice or musical instrument lessons in high school. Participation in music classes, choral groups, bands, and orchestras is also good preparation for a music teaching career.

Postsecondary Training
Like all musicians, music teachers spend years mastering their instruments or developing their voices. Private teachers need no formal training or licenses, but most have spent years studying with an experienced musician, either in a school or conservatory or through private lessons. Teachers in elementary schools and high schools must

have at least a bachelor's degree in music education as well as a state-issued teaching license. Approximately 600 conservatories, universities, and colleges offer bachelor's degrees in music education to qualify students for state certificates. The National Association of Schools of Music offers a directory of accredited music schools at its website, http://nasm.arts-accredit.org.

To teach music in colleges and schools of music or in conservatories, you generally need a graduate degree in music. Many teachers at this level also have doctorate degrees. However, very talented and well-known performers or composers are sometimes hired without any formal graduate training, but only a few people reach that level of fame.

Certification or Licensing

The Music Teachers National Association (MTNA) offers voluntary certification to music teachers who meet academic, performance, and teaching competencies and pass proficiency examinations in music theory, music history/literature, and/or pedagogy/teaching education. Upon fulfillment of these requirements, the applicant may use the nationally certified teacher of music designation. Contact the MTNA for more information on certification.

Elementary and secondary music teachers who work in public schools must be licensed under regulations established by the state in which they are teaching. If moving, teachers have to comply with any other regulations in their new state to be able to teach, though many states have reciprocity agreements that make it easier for teachers to change locations.

Licensure examinations test prospective teachers for competency in basic subjects such as reading, writing, teaching, and other subject matter. In addition, many states are moving toward a performance-based evaluation for licensing. In this case, after passing the teaching examination, prospective teachers are given provisional licenses. Only after proving themselves capable in the classroom are they eligible for a full license.

Another growing trend spurred by recent teacher shortages in elementary and high schools is alternative licensure arrangements. Some states are issuing provisional licenses to aspiring teachers who have bachelor's degrees but lack formal education courses and training in the classroom. These workers immediately begin teaching under the supervision of a licensed educator for one to two years and take education classes outside of their working hours. Once they have completed the required course work and gained experience in the classroom, they are granted a full license.

Other Requirements

Above all, music teachers must have a broad cultural knowledge and a love for music. They should be proficient with at least one musical instrument or demonstrate strong vocal ability. Many feel that the desire to teach is a calling. This calling is based on a love of learning. Teachers of young children and young adults must respect their students as individuals, with personalities, strengths, and weaknesses of their own. They must also be patient and self-disciplined to manage a large group independently. Because they work with students who are at very impressionable ages, music teachers should serve as good role models. Elementary and secondary teachers should also be well organized, as they have to keep track of the work and progress of many students.

If you aim to teach at the college level, you should enjoy reading, writing, researching, and performing. Not only will you spend many years studying in school, but your whole career will be based on communicating your thoughts and ideas. People skills are important because you'll be dealing directly with students, administrators, and other faculty members on a daily basis. You should feel comfortable in a role of authority and possess self-confidence in your teaching and musical abilities.

EXPLORING

To learn more about music and the career of music teacher, sing in your school or church choir or join a band or orchestra. Get as much experience as you can playing, singing, and performing. Read all you can about music theory, music history, famous musicians, and performance. Talk to your music teachers about what they like and don't like about teaching music. If you are a college student, you can become a student member of MTNA or MENC: The National Association for Music Education. As an MTNA collegiate member, you will receive *American Music Teacher*, a publication that provides useful information for music teachers, and opportunities to participate in performance competitions. Student members of MENC: The National Association for Music Education receive *Music Educators Journal* and *Teaching Music,* publications that offer articles on trends in music education, teaching approaches and philosophies, lesson plans, and technology as it relates to music education. MENC also offers many free and useful resources at its website, http://www.menc.org. Visitors can read free publications, such as *Careers in Music,* and participate in online open forums, which feature discussions of trends in music education, college training, and almost any other topic associated with music.

To gain general teaching experience, look for leadership opportunities that involve working with children. You might find summer work as a counselor in a summer music camp, as a leader of a scout troop, or as an assistant in a public park or community center. To get firsthand teaching experience, volunteer for a peer tutoring program. Many other teaching opportunities may exist in your community.

If you are interested in becoming a college professor, spend some time on a college campus to get a sense of the environment. Write to colleges for their admissions brochures and course catalogs (or check them out online). Read about the music faculty and the courses they teach. Before visiting college campuses, make arrangements to speak to professors who teach music courses that interest you. These professors may allow you to sit in on their classes and observe.

EMPLOYERS

There are more than 2.6 million elementary and secondary school teachers employed in the United States. Music teachers make up a very small percentage of this group. The largest number of teaching positions are available in urban or suburban areas, but career opportunities also exist in small towns. Music teachers are also finding opportunities in charter schools, which are smaller, deregulated schools that receive public funding.

There are approximately 58,000 college and university music, art, and drama professors in the United States. According to the U.S. Department of Labor, the following states have the highest concentrations of college music teachers: Massachusetts, Oklahoma, New Hampshire, and Rhode Island. With a doctorate, a number of publications or notable performances, and a record of good teaching, music professors should find opportunities in universities all across the country.

STARTING OUT

Elementary and secondary school music teachers can use their college placement offices and state departments of education to find job openings. Many local schools advertise teaching positions in newspapers. Another option is to directly contact the administration of the schools at which you'd like to work. While looking for a full-time position, you can work as a substitute teacher. In more urban areas with many schools, you may be able to find full-time substitute work.

Prospective college professors should start the process of finding a teaching position while in graduate school. You will need to develop a curriculum vitae (a detailed, academic resume), work on your academic writing, assist with research, attend conferences, demonstrate your musical ability, and gain teaching experience and recommendations. Because of the competition for tenure-track positions, you may have to work for a few years in temporary positions. Some professional associations maintain lists of teaching opportunities in their areas. They may also make lists of applicants available to college administrators looking to fill an available position. MENC: The National Association for Music Education offers job listings at its website. Association members can also register as job seekers at the site.

ADVANCEMENT

As elementary and secondary music teachers acquire experience or additional education, they earn higher wages and are assigned more responsibilities. Teachers with leadership skills and an interest in administrative work may advance to serve as principals or supervisors, though the number of these positions is limited, and competition for them is fierce. Another move may be into higher education, teaching music classes at a community college or university. For most of these positions, additional education is required. Other common career transitions are into related fields.

At the college level, the normal pattern of advancement is from instructor to assistant professor, to associate professor, to full professor. All four academic ranks are concerned primarily with teaching and research. College faculty members who have an interest in and a talent for administration may be advanced to chair of a department or to dean of their college. A few become college or university presidents or other types of administrators.

Private music teachers advance by establishing reputations as excellent teachers, which increases the number of students interested in studying with them.

EARNINGS

Music teachers earn a wide range of salaries based on their level of expertise, geographic location, whether they work full or part time, and other factors. According to the National Association for Music Education, early childhood music educators earn $6 to $60/hour, while studio music teachers earn $10 to $100/hour. Full-time music teachers at the elementary and secondary levels earn salaries that range from $19,000 to $70,000 annually.

College professors' earnings vary depending on their academic department, the size of the school, the type of school (public, private, women's only, etc.), and the level of position the professor holds. The U.S. Department of Labor reports that college music, art, and drama teachers earned median annual salaries of $47,560 in 2002. The lowest paid teachers in this group earned less than $24,780, and the highest paid earned $85,620 or more annually. Postsecondary music teachers in New York, California, Delaware, Connecticut, and New Jersey earned the highest salaries.

WORK ENVIRONMENT

Most elementary and secondary school music teachers are contracted to work 10 months out of the year, with a two-month vacation during the summer. During their summer break, many continue their education to renew or upgrade their teaching licenses and earn higher salaries. Teachers in schools that operate year-round work eight-week sessions with one-week breaks in between and a five-week vacation in the winter.

Music teachers work in generally pleasant conditions, although some older schools may have poor heating or electrical systems. The work can seem confining, requiring them to remain in the classroom throughout most of the day. Elementary school teachers have to deal with energetic children all day, which can be tiring and trying.

Elementary and high school hours are generally 8:00 A.M. to 3:00 P.M., but music teachers employed in this setting may work more than 40 hours a week teaching, preparing for classes, grading papers or performances, and directing extracurricular activities. They may also be required to teach non-music related classes and supervise study halls and lunches. Similarly, most college music teachers work more than 40 hours each week. Although they may teach only two or three classes a semester, they spend many hours preparing for class, examining student work, and conducting research.

Studio teachers and early childhood music educators usually teach part time, with the remainder of their work hours filled with a second job as a musician or another career. This type of work arrangement allows them considerable flexibility in regard to their schedule. Studio teachers who own their own businesses must spend a considerable amount of time handling business matters such as invoicing, billing, and soliciting new customers.

OUTLOOK

After decades of program declines, music education is regaining popularity in U.S. schools. In 2000, a Gallup Poll found that 93 percent

of Americans believe that music should be part of school curricula—
a 5 percent increase from 1997. As a result, career opportunities in
teaching music are expected to be good at the elementary and secondary levels. The National Education Association believes that it
will be a challenge to hire enough new elementary and secondary
school teachers to meet rising enrollments and replace the large number of retiring teachers, primarily because of low teacher salaries.
Although music programs are on the rebound in many schools, some
public schools facing severe budget problems are still eliminating
music programs, making competition for jobs at these schools even
keener. In addition, private music teachers are facing greater competition from instrumental musicians who increasingly must turn to
teaching because of the oversupply of musicians seeking playing jobs.

Though the *Occupational Outlook Handbook* predicts faster-
than-average employment growth for college and university professors over the next several years, college music teachers will experience
strong competition for full-time, tenure-track positions at four-year
schools. Music educators who aspire to teach at the college level will
enjoy the strongest employment prospects at community colleges.

FOR MORE INFORMATION

For information on issues that affect college teachers, contact
American Association of University Professors
1012 14th Street, NW, Suite 500
Washington, DC 20005
Tel: 202-737-5900
http://www.aaup.org

For information on union membership and earnings, contact
American Federation of Teachers
555 New Jersey Avenue, NW
Washington, DC 20001
Tel: 202-879-4400
http://www.aft.org

The CMS is a consortium of college, university, conservatory, and
independent musicians and scholars interested in all aspects of music
and music teaching. Visit its website for a directory of U.S. and
Canadian music programs and statistics on music education.
The College Music Society (CMS)
312 East Pine Street
Missoula, MT 59802

Tel: 406-721-9616
http://www.music.org

For information on student membership and certification, contact
Music Teachers National Association
441 Vine Street, Suite 505
Cincinnati, OH 45202
Tel: 888-512-5278
http://www.mtna.org

To participate in online forums about music education and to read a variety of useful online brochures, such as Careers in Music *and* How to Nail a College Entrance Audition, *visit the following website:*
MENC: The National Association for Music Education
1806 Robert Fulton Drive
Reston, VA 20191
Tel: 800-336-3768
http://www.menc.org

For information on choosing a music school and a database of accredited music schools in the United States, visit the NASM website.
National Association of Schools of Music (NASM)
11250 Roger Bacon Drive, Suite 21
Reston, VA 20190-5248
Tel: 703-437-0700
http://nasm.arts-accredit.org

For information on teacher accreditation, contact
National Council for Accreditation of Teacher Education
2010 Massachusetts Avenue, NW, Suite 500
Washington, DC 20036
Tel: 202-466-7496
http://www.ncate.org

The NEA is a membership organization for public school teachers at all academic levels.
National Education Association (NEA)
1201 16th Street, NW
Washington, DC 20036
Tel: 202-833-4000
http://www.nea.org

INTERVIEW

Ann Boyle has been a music teacher at Near North Montessori School in Chicago, Illinois, for three years. She spoke with the editors of Careers in Focus: Music *about her career.*

Q. What are your primary and secondary job duties?

A. My primary job duties are teaching general music to students in first through sixth grade, as well as private individual voice lessons. My secondary job duties are not music related; I supervise seventh and eighth grade students eating lunch.

Q. What are the benefits of the Montessori philosophy?

A. Montessori education differs from traditional education in that each class has a combination of age groups. For example, my class of six- through nine-year-olds is evenly divided between the age groups. The multi-age classes allow older kids to act as leaders and helpers to the younger children. It also allows for more flexibility in the learning environment. In this setting, more advanced younger kids have more opportunities to work with older kids who are closer to their learning level. In traditional educational settings, children are the same age, and class lessons are largely standardized. Students have less opportunity to get out on their own and learn creatively.

Q. Please describe an average day.

A. I begin my workday at noon by supervising students at lunch. Then I teach recorder to about 10 students. From 1:00 to 3:00 P.M., I teach 18 students general music. This could be playing instruments (percussion instruments such as xylophones and drums) or singing, talking about, or listening to music. I teach private voice lessons after the official school day ends.

Q. How did you train for this job?

A. I received a bachelor's degree in music from DePaul University in Chicago, and a master's degree in music (with an emphasis on the performance of early music) from the University of Indiana-Bloomington.

To prepare myself for teaching at this school, I took a two-week course that covered the Carl Orff teaching philosophy. Orff was a German composer and educator whose philosophy of music education is popular throughout the world.

Q. How can a recent graduate find a job in this field?

A. Music education is more focused than many disciplines. Most students in this major plan to teach music. Colleges are very attuned to this and arrange their programs to include student teaching and preparation for certification, which creates good employment opportunities. Many students utilize job-placement resources in their music department or at their university's career center. Some students even get temporary jobs at their school upon graduation.

Graduates can also view job listings at online educator sites, such as HigherEdJobs.com. Some of these sites are free, while others require a subscription. They can also check local newspapers for positions.

Q. What are the most important personal and professional qualities for music teachers?

A. First and foremost, you need to concentrate on being the best musician you can be. Then you must have patience and a love for children.

Q. What are some of the pros and cons of being a music teacher?

A. At Near North Montessori, I have the freedom to do whatever I want as far as curriculum and material, so that is a major pro.

Working with kids can be draining, but breaks, holidays, and summer vacations allow you to stay refreshed.

Q. What advice would you give college students as they graduate and look for jobs in this field?

A. My advice for aspiring music teachers is to try out the career before you decide to make a commitment. Try to get an assistant position before you go through the certification process—which will require a considerable investment of time and money.

You should also be as flexible and patient as possible. Be open to any and all possibilities to get your foot in the door. If you have trouble finding a job at a school, look to churches, neighborhood organizations, park districts, the YMCA, or other similar organizations that offer part-time teaching opportunities that will help you gain experience.

Q. What is the future employment outlook for music educators?

A. Music is one of the first things to be cut from a school's budget, so sometimes it can be difficult to find—and keep—full-time employment. Studies have shown that music and music education enhance math and language abilities. Many schools are now introducing arts integration programs where music or art activities are used to enhance the learning of an unrelated subject such as math. Opportunities should remain steady as long as music education budgets aren't reduced and schools continue to use music as a tool to enhance others types of learning.

Music Therapists

OVERVIEW

Music therapists treat and rehabilitate people with mental, physical, and emotional disabilities. They use the creative process of music in their therapy sessions to determine the underlying causes of problems and to help patients achieve therapeutic goals. The specific objectives of the therapeutic activities vary according to the needs of the patient and the setting of the therapy program. There are approximately 5,000 music therapists employed in the United States.

HISTORY

Creative arts therapy programs are fairly recent additions to the health care field. Although many theories of mental and physical therapy have existed for centuries, it has been only in the last 70 years or so that health care professionals have truly realized the healing powers of music and other forms of artistic self-expression.

According to the American Music Therapy Association (AMTA), the discipline of music therapy began during World War I, when amateur and professional musicians visited veteran's hospitals to play for the thousands of veterans who were being treated for both physical and emotional maladies caused by the war. Health administrators and physicians hired music therapists as they began to recognize that the music positively affected their patients. The field of music therapy advanced further during and after World War II, when the Department of Veterans Affairs (VA) developed and organized various music and other creative-arts activities for patients in VA hospitals. These activities had a dramatic effect on the physical and mental well-being of the veterans, and music and other creative arts therapists began to help treat and reha-bilitate patients in other health care settings.

As music therapy grew in popularity, it became evident that for-mal training was needed for music therapists to be most effective. The first music therapy degree program was founded at Michigan State University in 1944. Today, there are more than 70 AMTA-approved music therapy programs in the United States.

In 1998, the AMTA was founded as a result of a merger between the National Association for Music Therapy and the American Association for Music Therapy. Its oversight of educational programs ensures the professional integrity of music therapists working in the field.

THE JOB

Similar to dreaming, creative-arts therapy taps into the subconscious and gives people a mode of expression in an uncensored environment. This is important because before patients can begin to heal, they must first identify their feelings. Once they recognize their feelings, they can begin to develop an understanding of the relationship between their feelings and their behavior.

Music therapists use musical lessons and activities to improve a patient's self-confidence and self-awareness, to relieve states of depres-sion, and to improve physical dexterity. For example, a music thera-pist treating a patient with Alzheimer's disease might play songs from the patient's past in order to stimulate long- and short-term memory, soothe feelings of agitation, and increase a sense of reality. A musi-cal therapist treating a patient with a physical disability may have the patient play a keyboard or xylophone to improve their dexterity or have them walk to a musical selection to improve their balance and gait. Music therapists also treat people with mental health needs, learning and developmental disabilities, physical disabilities, brain injuries, conditions related to aging, alcohol and drug abuse prob-lems, and acute and chronic pain.

The main goal of a music therapist is to improve the client's phys-ical, mental, and emotional health. Before therapists begin any treat-ment, they meet with a team of other health care professionals. After determining the strengths, limitations, and interests of their client, they create a program to promote positive change and growth. The music therapist continues to confer with the other health care work-ers as the program progresses and adjusts the program according to the client's response to the therapy.

Patients undergoing music therapy do not need to have any spe-cial musical ability or be open to one particular musical style. Of course, the patient's personal therapy preferences, physical and mental circumstances, and his or her taste in music (such as a fondness for rap, classical, or country music) will all affect how the music therapist treats the patient.

Music therapists work with all age groups: young children, adolescents, adults, and senior citizens. They work in individual, group, and family sessions. The therapist's approach, however, depends on the specific needs of the client or group.

Some music therapists may also edit or write publications about music or creative-arts therapy, teach music therapy courses at colleges and universities, work as professional musicians, or specialize in other creative-arts therapy careers such as art, dance, or drama therapy.

REQUIREMENTS

High School

To become a creative arts therapist, you will need a bachelor's degree, so take a college preparatory curriculum while in high school. You should become as proficient as possible with music, musical

Books about Music Therapy

Benward, Bruce, and Gary White. *Music in Theory and Practice.* 7th ed. Boston: McGraw-Hill Humanities, 2003.

Davis, William, Kate Gfeller, and Michael Thaut. *An Introduction to Music Therapy: Theory and Practice.* 2d ed. Boston: McGraw-Hill Humanities, 1999.

Gaynor, Mitchell. *The Healing Power of Sound: Recovery from Life-Threatening Illness Using, Sound, Voice, and Music.* Boston: Shambhala Publications, 2002.

Hanser, Suzanne. *The New Music Therapist's Handbook.* 2d ed. Boston: Berklee Press, 2000.

Hodges, Donald, ed. *Handbook of Music Psychology.* 2d ed. St. Louis: MMB Music, 1996.

Peters, Jacqueline. *Music Therapy: An Introduction.* 2d ed. Springfield, Ill.: Charles C. Thomas, 2000.

Wigram, Tony. *A Comprehensive Guide to Music Therapy: Theory, Clinical Practice, Research and Training.* London: Jessica Kingsley Publishers, 2003.

instruments, and musical theory. When therapists work with patients, they must be able to concentrate completely on the patient rather than on learning how to use tools or techniques. A good starting point for an aspiring music therapist is to study piano or guitar.

In addition to courses such as drama, music, and English, you should consider taking introductory classes in psychology. Also, communications classes will give you an understanding of the various ways people communicate, both verbally and nonverbally.

Postsecondary Training
To become a music therapist you must earn at least a bachelor's degree in music therapy. There are more than 70 AMTA-approved college and university music therapy programs in the United States. Typical courses in a bachelor's degree program in music therapy include professional music therapy, music therapy theory, assessment, evaluation, populations served, ethics, and research and clinical interventions. Undergraduates will also take supporting courses in music, psychology, and human physiology.

In most cases, however, you will also need a graduate degree to advance in the field. Graduate school admissions requirements vary by program, so you should contact the graduate programs you are interested in to find out about their admissions policies. For some fields, you may be required to submit a portfolio of your work along with the written application. The AMTA provides a list of schools that meet its quality standards at its website, http://www.musictherapy.org/handbook/schools.html.

In graduate school, your study of psychology and music will be in-depth. Classes for someone seeking a master's in music therapy may include group psychotherapy, foundation of creativity theory, assessment and treatment planning, and music therapy presentation. In addition to classroom study, you will complete an internship or supervised practicum (that is, work with clients). Depending on your program, you may also need to write a thesis or present a final artistic project before receiving your degree.

Certification or Licensing
Students who receive a bachelor's degree in music therapy are eligible to sit for a certification examination offered by the Certification Board for Music Therapists. Therapists who successfully complete this examination may use the music therapist-board certified designation. Music therapists are required to renew this certification every five years by completing continuing education credits or by retaking the certification exam.

Many music therapists hold additional licenses in other fields, such as social work, education, mental health, or marriage and family therapy. In some states, music therapists need to be licensed depending on their place of work. For specific information on licensing, you will need to check with your state's licensing board. Music therapists are also often members of other professional associations, including the American Psychological Association, the American Association of Marriage and Family Therapists, and the American Counseling Association.

Other Requirements

To succeed as a music therapist, you should have a background in and a love of music. You should also have a strong desire to help others seek positive change in their lives. You must be able to work well with other people—both patients and other health professionals—in the development and implementation of therapy programs. You must have the patience and the stamina to teach and practice therapy with patients for whom progress is often very slow. A therapist must always keep in mind that even a tiny amount of progress might be extremely significant for some patients and their families. A good sense of humor is also a valuable trait.

EXPLORING

To learn more about careers in music therapy, visit the website of the AMTA. Talk with people working in the music therapy field and try to arrange to observe a music therapy session. Look for part-time or summer jobs, or volunteer at a hospital, clinic, nursing home, or any of a number of health care facilities. You might also consider becoming a student member of the AMTA. As a membership benefit, you will receive association publications such as the *Journal of Music Therapy* and *Music Therapy Perspectives*.

A summer job as an aide at a camp for disabled children, for example, may help provide insight into the nature of music therapy, including both its rewards and its demands. Such experience can be very valuable in deciding if you are suited to handle the inherent frustrations of a therapy career.

EMPLOYERS

Music therapists usually work as members of an interdisciplinary health care team that may include physicians, nurses, social workers, psychiatrists, and psychologists. Although often employed in medical and psychiatric hospitals, therapists also work in rehabilitation centers, nursing homes, day treatment facilities, shelters for battered women, pain and stress management clinics, substance abuse programs, hospices, and correctional facilities. Others maintain their own private practices. Some music therapists work with children in grammar and high schools, either as therapists or as music teachers. Others teach or conduct research in the creative arts at colleges and universities.

STARTING OUT

Unpaid training internships (see the AMTA website for a list of internship opportunities) or assistantships that students complete during study for a bachelor's degree in music therapy often can lead to a first job in the field. Graduates can use the placement offices at their colleges or universities to help them find positions in the field. AMTA members can also access a list of job openings at the association's website.

Music therapists who are new to the field might consider doing volunteer work at a nonprofit community organization, correctional facility, or neighborhood association to gain some practical experience. Therapists who want to start their own practice can host group therapy sessions in their homes. Music therapists may also wish to associate with other members of the alternative health care field in order to gain experience and build a client base.

ADVANCEMENT

With experience, music therapists can move into supervisory, administrative, and teaching positions. Often, the supervision of interns can resemble a therapy session. The interns will discuss their feelings and ask questions they may have regarding their work with clients. How did they handle their clients? What were the reactions to what their clients said or did? What could they be doing to help more? The supervising therapist helps the interns become competent music therapists.

EARNINGS

Salaries for music therapists vary based on experience, level of training, and education. Music therapists earned average annual salaries of $34,893 in 2000, according to the AMTA. Salaries varied from that average by region, most by less than $2,000 a year, with the highest average salary reported in the New England states at $41,600. Salaries reported by AMTA members ranged from $15,000 to

$81,000. Music therapists with more than 20 years of professional experience earned $43,306 in 2000.

According to MENC: The National Association for Music Education, music therapists earn the following annual salaries based on employment setting: hospital-psychiatric facility, $20,000–$62,000; special education facility, $22,000–$42,000; clinic for disabled children, $15,000–$70,000; mental health center, $21,000–$65,000; nursing home, $17,000–$65,000; correctional facility, $23,000–$58,000; and private practice, $18,000–$77,000.

Music therapists in private practice must provide their own benefits, including health insurance.

WORK ENVIRONMENT

Music therapists work a typical 40-hour, five-day workweek; at times, however, they may have to work extra hours. The number of patients under a therapist's care depends on their specific employment setting. Although many therapists work in hospitals, they may also be employed in such facilities as clinics, rehabilitation centers, children's homes, schools, and nursing homes. Some therapists maintain service contracts with several facilities. For instance, a therapist might work two days a week at a hospital, one day at a nursing home, and the rest of the week at a rehabilitation center. This type of work arrangement entails frequent travel from location to location to see patients.

Most buildings are pleasant, comfortable, and clean places in which to work. Experienced music therapists might choose to be self-employed, working with patients in their own studios. In such a case, the therapist might work more irregular hours to accommodate patient schedules. Other therapists might maintain a combination of service contract work with one or more facilities in addition to a private caseload of clients referred to them by other health care professionals. Whether therapists work on service contracts with various facilities or maintain private practices, they must handle all of the business and administrative details and worries that go along with being self-employed.

OUTLOOK

The AMTA predicts a promising future for the field of music therapy. Demand for music therapists will increase as medical professionals and the general public become aware of the benefits gained through music therapy. Although enrollment in college therapy programs is increasing, new graduates are usually able to find jobs. In cases where an individual is unable to find a full-time position, a therapist might obtain service contracts for part-time work at several facilities.

Job openings in facilities such as nursing homes should continue to increase as the elderly population grows over the next few decades. Advances in medical technology and the recent practice of early discharge from hospitals should also create new opportunities in managed care facilities, chronic pain clinics, cancer care facilities, and hospices. The demand for music therapists should continue to increase as more people become aware of the need to help disabled and ill patients in creative ways.

FOR MORE INFORMATION

For comprehensive information about the career of music therapist and a list of approved educational programs, contact
American Music Therapy Association
8455 Colesville Road, Suite 1000
Silver Spring, MD 20910
Tel: 301-589-3300
http://www.musictherapy.org

For information on certification, contact
Certification Board for Music Therapists
506 East Lancaster Avenue, Suite 102
Downingtown, PA 19335
Tel: 800-765-2268
http://www.cbmt.org

For information on music therapy at the international level, visit the following website
World Federation for Music Therapy
http://www.musictherapyworld.net

─────────── INTERVIEW ───────────

Michele Erich has been a music therapist in Wilmington, North Carolina, for 15 years. She spoke to the editors of Careers in Focus: Music *about her career.*

Q. What are your primary and secondary job duties?
A. I provide music therapy (MT) individual sessions at a medical center that focuses on pediatrics, surgical trauma intensive

care, and adult cancer. I assess patient needs, implement session interventions, document progress, and communicate with the medical team. Other tasks that I am responsible for include assisting with the budget, billing requirements, and maintaining supplies.

I also work with volunteers and students doing volunteer work and internship training and coordinate a Healing Arts Network of contracted practitioners (massage, art, dance, horticulture, and energy therapists).

Q. What is a session intervention?

A. Session interventions are the therapy we offer to patients. They involve singing or writing a song, listening to music, playing a musical instrument, improvising music, analyzing song lyrics, or any other technique that helps a patient. For example, I might sing songs with a three-year-old who is about to have an IV administered. The singing calms her down and gets her thinking about something else other than the IV. Or I may use a song that teaches a concept (such as the ABCs) to teach a child who is having trouble learning the alphabet.

Q. How did you train for this job? What was your college major?

A. I received both a bachelor's and master's degree from East Carolina University. As part of this training, I completed practicums and internships.

Q. Please describe your internship.

A. I had a six-month internship with developmentally disabled residents of a long-term residential facility. It was a culmination of working with clients in different settings. I was able to apply my musical and therapeutic skills, as well as my practicum experiences, to a different population. The clients were very receptive to working with me; they had been working with music therapists for years. Overall, the internship provided a supportive learning environment.

Q. How/where did you get your first job in this field? What did you do?

A. I was hired by a private psychiatric hospital in Jacksonville, North Carolina. I provided music therapy for children and adolescents hospitalized for psychiatric treatment and led both group and individual sessions.

Q. **What kind of sources were—and are—available to some-one looking to get into this field?**

A. The American Music Therapy Association (AMTA) has great resources and services along with regional and state MT organizations connected with AMTA. I found out about MT from my high school band director.

Q. **What are the most important personal and professional qualities for music therapists?**

A. Music therapists should be creative, organized, flexible, energetic, kind, approachable (friendly), and caring. They should be good musicians and have strong counseling skills, verbal and written skills, and be good listeners.

Q. **What are some of the pros and cons of your job?**

A. **Pros**

- Being able to help individuals through music

- Being able to make a connection with a patient/client that can't be reached through other methods

- Being able to offer a helpful intervention that doesn't produce negative side effects

Con

- Lack of awareness of the benefits of the music therapy profession by employers and insurance companies

Q. **What advice would you offer college students as they graduate and look for jobs in this field?**

A. Be flexible but true to your training, and believe in the power of music therapy.

Music Venue Owners and Managers

OVERVIEW

Music venue owners and managers are responsible for the overall success of a music venue. They book music acts, oversee employees, and play a role in the hiring and firing of staff. While owners have the final say in the club's business decisions, managers handle the daily operations of the venue, such as hiring, training, and scheduling staff members, planning music programming, checking music and bar equipment, and ensuring the safety and cleanliness of the club.

HISTORY

Formal music venues have been around in many different forms for centuries. Cathedrals and other religious buildings served as some of the earliest venues. But the music venue of today is more recent; the emergence of rock and roll in the mid-1950s had much to do with the evolution of the music club as an entertainment destination.

During the first half of the 20th century, popular music was dominated by big-band jazz. People gathered to hear these large music ensembles in ballrooms, hotels, and other large facilities. Soon, however, solo performers with roots in gospel, blues, folk, and country broke new ground in music, and the result was the birth of rock. This music required a venue different than those used by the big bands. Music venues of all sizes sprang up across the country, from blues clubs in Chicago, to bluegrass clubs in the Appalachian region to rock clubs in New York City. Today, hundreds of music venues of all sizes can be found in major cities, and small towns typically host a few music halls as well. The popularity of music as live entertainment has driven this growth and will continue to expand the number and scope of music venues across the country.

THE JOB

In general terms, music venue managers, like other facility managers, coordinate the events that occur in the club with the services and people who make those events possible. This involves booking bands, hiring and firing workers when needed, and overseeing electrical workers, sound technicians, bar staff, security guards, and other employees that keep the club running. Depending on the size of the music venue, managers may have different job titles and specialized duties, such as sound manager or restaurant and bar manager.

Larger music venues may contract work to outside vendors. This may include security, food and drink services, or electrical work. It is the responsibility of the music venue manager to hire such contractors and to monitor the quality of their work.

Finally, it is the manager's duty to make certain that the music venue, its workers, and the services offered are in accordance with federal, state, and local regulations.

Music venue owners are concerned with much more than the internal workings of the club. They must be sure they have the proper finances to open a club and keep it running. This may require months, if not years, of research and long-term financial planning. Another crucial issue owners must consider is how their club compares to others in the area. Are ticket prices reasonable? Does the venue offer enough seating or space for patrons to dance? Is the club safe for concertgoers? To determine these answers, owners may visit other music venues to investigate their design, organization, and music schedule.

In general, music venue owners and managers spend most of their time in their office or within the club itself, supervising the day-to-day management of the facility. Club owners determine the organizational structure of the facility and set staffing requirements. As staffing needs arise, the manager addresses them with the owner, who then sets the education, experience, and performance standards for each position. Depending on the size of the venue, hiring may be conducted by a separate personnel director. However, in most small music clubs, the manager is usually the one to sift through stacks of resumes whenever a position opens up. Usually, the manager determines all policies and procedures having to do with the morale, safety, service, appearance, and performance of venue employees.

REQUIREMENTS

High School

To prepare for this line of work, recommended high school courses include music, business, mathematics, and computer science. Speech and writing classes will help you hone your communication skills. Managing a school club (such as a traveling band or chorus) or other organization will give you an introduction to overseeing budgets and the work of others.

Postsecondary Training

These days, a bachelor's degree is pretty much required to enter the field of music facility management. Although in the past it wasn't necessary, the complexity of running the venue and the competition for jobs has made a college degree nearly mandatory. In fact, in many instances, a master's degree in facility management or business is preferred. Some schools offer degrees in music industry or facility management. However, any degree that emphasizes strong business and finance skills will be useful. Visit the website of The College Music Society (http://www.music.org) for information on educational paths.

Regardless of your educational background, the strongest selling point you can have in the music business is experience. Previous work at a successful club will help you more than an advanced degree.

Certification or Licensing

At the moment, certification in facility management is not mandatory, but it is becoming a distinguishing credential among the managers of the largest, most profitable venues. Put simply, a music venue can bring its owners a lot of revenue, and these owners aren't willing to trust the management to individuals who are not qualified to run them. Certification is one way a club owner can ensure that certain industry standards in facility management are met. The International Facility Management Association (IFMA), probably the industry leader in certification, offers the designation certified facility manager. The International Association of Assembly Managers (IAAM) also offers the certification designation certified facilities executive. For contact information for these associations, see the end of this article.

Other Requirements

Most music venue owners require that higher level managers have a minimum of five years of experience in the music or management industry. This may include experience in other manager positions or in related music careers. Many managers end up in their management positions after first working as one of the venue's staff members, such as one of the club's regular musicians or sound managers.

In addition to experience, both owners and managers need to be strong communicators to work well with staff and relate well to the club's patrons. They need to be able to clearly and concisely state their ideas, information about facility operations, and goals about running the venue and always be willing to help promote business.

Venue owners, in particular, need to possess excellent strategic, budgetary, and operational planning skills to keep the club in business and to ensure profits. The owner's decisions affect all operations within the music venue, so the owner needs to be capable of making the right choices and have the ability to juggle many different tasks.

One often overlooked quality that both owners and managers should have is an appreciation for all kinds of music. They should also have the ability to listen to the public and be mindful of current music trends. By paying attention to the venue's demographics and constantly looking for new and emerging bands that fit their usual clientele, owners and managers can expect to book talent that will sell out shows.

EXPLORING

Become actively involved in band or chorus while in school. To manage or own a club, you should be familiar with music and what makes music good. To gain experience in business administration and management, volunteer to help coordinate school plays, band or choral performances, or any other production. Any and all experience helps, beginning with organizing and managing band equipment, for example, to working as a stage manager for school plays.

Part-time or summer jobs as stagehands, ushers, or other positions are available at theaters, outdoor music festivals, and other venues. Many music shows are held in bars and other facilities catering to the over-21 crowd, so be prepared to look elsewhere for opportunities while you are underage.

College students interested in music facility management can often locate valuable internships through contacts they have developed from part-time jobs, but their college placement centers can also help to line up internships.

Professional organizations within the field also sponsor opportunities to learn on-the-job. The IAAM offers internships to qualified students. Typically, participating facilities that serve as sites for IAAM internships are responsible for the selection of their interns. While some of these facilities aren't specifically geared toward music shows, much of the management skills and responsibilities are shared and will provide you with a wonderful opportunity to learn firsthand.

EMPLOYERS

There are thousands of music venues, from small clubs to stadium arenas, located all over the country. Large metropolitan areas such as New York, Los Angeles, San Francisco, and Chicago offer the most opportunities to break into the music management business, but these jobs can also be the hardest to get. Management positions in small towns may be fewer, but the competition for positions will not be as fierce.

STARTING OUT

Graduates of programs in music facility management usually find jobs through internships, from personal contacts they developed in the field, or from job listings in their college's career-placement departments.

Keep in mind that the jobs of general manager (and especially club owner) are not entry-level jobs. Managers might start out in other positions within the music venue and work their way up to a management position. Other managers and owners move into the music business after first working in other industries. For example, a business manager with a background and passion for music might decide to give up the corporate world to operate or purchase a music club.

ADVANCEMENT

Experience and certification are the best ways for someone to advance within the ranks of music venue management. Years of successful, on-the-job experience count for a great deal in this industry. Club owners look for managers who have demonstrated the ability to run a venue smoothly and profitably. Certification is another way in which success can be gauged. Since certification goes hand in hand with experience, it is assumed that those individuals who are certified are the best in the field.

Beyond experience and certification, a willingness and eagerness to adapt to music trends and branch into new areas is another important factor affecting advancement. The most successful managers and owners are willing to embrace new sounds as well as changing technology that will improve the operation of their clubs.

Club managers advance by moving to larger clubs with bigger budgets and more popular bands. Owners advance their careers by running successful, profitable businesses.

EARNINGS

Earnings for music venue owners and managers depend on their experience and education, as well as the size and success of their club. General and operations managers (the category under which the U.S. Department of Labor classifies small business managers and owners) earned median annual salaries of $68,210 in 2002. The lowest paid 10 percent earned less than $32,700, and the highest paid 10 percent earned $104,970 or more per year. Club managers and owners who are certified earn higher salaries than those who are not certified. The IFMA reports that members who hold the certified facility manager designation earn an average of $8,000 more than their noncertified counterparts.

WORK ENVIRONMENT

One of the perks of this profession is the glamorous atmosphere of the music industry; venue owners and managers get to meet musicians, sometimes listen to music before its released, and decide which bands will fit with their venue. Although their work is most often done behind the scenes, they may have indirect or direct contact with the high-profile personalities who perform in clubs. In other words, music venue owners and managers work in interesting and entertaining surroundings. However, their jobs can be stressful and often require the ability to juggle many tasks at once. Managers and owners must constantly deal with the challenge of balancing the needs of staff members with the needs of the club's patrons—needs that may, at times, be at odds with each other.

Depending on the size of the music venue, the workload of owners and managers often requires them to work more than 40 hours a week. For managers, overtime is generally compensated by additional pay or time off. For owners, extra hours go unpaid; overtime simply comes with the territory of running a business. Because of the nature of entertainment venues, work hours are concentrated on nights and weekends, so time off is usually during the day and early week.

OUTLOOK

The U.S. Department of Labor predicts average growth for the music industry in general. Employment in music venues depends largely on the state of the economy. During slow periods of economic growth, people are less likely to spend money on concerts and other entertainment options, and clubs hire fewer workers to reduce costs.

However, this might affect the large venues (with higher ticket and concession prices) more than the small clubs. Even with a sluggish economy, most people will still have an appreciation for music and enough money to see a local artist or group play at a nearby venue.

FOR MORE INFORMATION

For information on becoming a certified facilities executive, contact
International Association of Assembly Managers
635 Fritz Drive, Suite 100
Coppell, TX 75019
Tel: 972-906-7441
http://www.iaam.org

For information on other certification options, contact
International Facility Management Association
1 East Greenway Plaza, Suite 1100
Houston, TX 77046
Tel: 713-623-4362
http://www.ifma.org

For school listings and other resources on the music industry, contact
The College Music Society
312 East Pine Street
Missoula, MT 59802
Tel: 406-721-9616
http://www.music.org

For more information on careers in music, contact
MENC: The National Association for Music Education
1806 Robert Fulton Drive
Reston, VA 20191
Tel: 800-336-3768
http://www.menc.org

Music Video Directors and Producers

QUICK FACTS

School Subjects
Business
Computer science
Music

Personal Skills
Artistic
Communication/ideas
Leadership/management

Work Environment
Indoors and outdoors
Primarily multiple locations

Minimum Education Level
High school diploma

Salary Range
$23,300 to $75,440 to
$119,760+

Certification or Licensing
None available

Outlook
Faster than the average

DOT
143, 187

GOE
01.02.03, 01.03.01

NOC
5121, 5131

O*NET-SOC
27-2012.01, 27-2012.02

OVERVIEW

"Lights! Camera! Action!" aptly summarizes the major responsibilities of the *music video director*. Directors are well known for their part in guiding actors, but they are involved in much more—casting, costuming, cinematography, lighting, editing, and sound recording. Music video directors must have insight into the many tasks that go into the creation of a music video, and they must have a broad vision of how each part will contribute to the final product.

Music video producers often work with the music video director by overseeing the budget, production schedule, and other tasks associated with music video production. There are nearly 30,000 directors and producers employed in the television, video, cable, and motion picture industries.

HISTORY

Music videos gained popular, mainstream appeal when MTV, the first all-music cable channel, was formed in 1981. But music videos have actually been around more than 100 years. In 1890, George Thomas, a photographer, created the first live-model illustrated song. Set to the song "The Little Lost Child," this series of photographic images printed on glass slides (and backed by live singers and musicians) hit vaudeville stages, and later, movie theaters. Customers lined up to see the shows. Suddenly, a new music sub-industry was born: illustrating popular songs to help sell sheet music.

The first music videos, called Soundies, were developed in the 1940s. They were composed of footage of a band or a solo singer simply performing a song on a stage. Soundies were used to promote artists (usually jazz musicians, but also torch singers, dancers, and comedians) as videos are used today.

Richard Lester is considered to be the father of contemporary music video. His exuberant, full-length films in the mid-1960s with The Beatles, such as *A Hard Day's Night* and *Help!,* were groundbreaking explorations of music and storytelling. Many of the musical segments in these movies were precursors to styles that we see in today's music videos. In fact, MTV took notice of Lester's work by presenting him with an award for his contributions to the art of music video in the 1980s.

Michael Nesmith, a member of the rock group The Monkees, is largely credited with creating the first music videos of the modern era. He made short, musical films for the television show *Saturday Night Live* in 1979, and the first video album, *Elephant Parts,* in 1981. The art form grew quickly in the 1980s with the popularity of MTV, which played music videos 24 hours a day, seven days a week. Most recording artists released music videos for their singles to generate interest in and sales for their latest albums.

The music video industry has come a long way from George Thomas's live-model illustrated songs. Advances such as computer-generated animation, digital filming, and digital sound have given music video directors more tools to work with and the ability to produce an increasing variety of looks, sounds, and characters in their finished videos. One constant remains from Thomas's days: music videos still play a major role in helping companies sell products such as sheet music, CDs, music videos, and concert tickets.

THE JOB

Music video directors and producers often work together as a team to create music videos for record companies and other employers. (Occasionally, a director may be responsible for all of the producer's tasks.) Though the director and producer work as a team, they generally approach their collaborative effort from two distinct vantage points. In short, the director is concerned with issues such as the look, feel, and sound of the video. Directors bear the ultimate responsibility for the tone and quality of the videos they work on. They are involved in preproduction (before the shoot), production (during the shoot), and postproduction (after the shoot). The producer is concerned with more practical concerns such as electricity, logistics, and business-related issues.

To be considered for jobs, music video directors and producers must present a bid (a written estimate of how much money they will need to shoot and complete the video) and a treatment to music recording executives, most often a video commissioner or marketing director. A treatment is a written overview of what a director plans to do in the music video. This is the director's only opportunity to convince music industry executives that he or she is the right person for the job. Some music video directors write only one treatment for a video, while others write three or more treatments and choose what they think is the best one for submission. Music video treatments are typically two pages long and answer questions such as the following: How will the video look and feel? What story will the video tell to viewers? Will the video feature music performance only, a story only, or a combination of the two? What type of medium will be used to shoot the music video: 16 mm film, 35 mm film, video, or a combination of several formats? During this time the director and producer meet with the *music video editor,* who shares their vision about the music video. They discuss the objectives of the video and the best way to present the artist's image, including settings, scenes, special effects, costumes, and camera angles.

After the director and producer submit the treatment, record industry executives review it and suggest revisions based on the project's budget and stylistic concerns. The director and producer then submit a revised treatment that is reviewed, and eventually approved, by the video commissioner, marketing director, music artist's manager, and the artist. Once a treatment is accepted, the director and producer begin work on the music video within days or weeks.

Music video directors are responsible for many tasks before and during the shoot. They interpret the stories and narratives presented in scripts and coordinate the filming of their interpretations. To do this, the director creates a shooting script and storyboards as a guide to assist in making the video. Music video directors must audition, select, and rehearse the acting crew, which may include dancers, actors, stunt performers, and backup musicians, as well as work closely with the musical artist in the video. They oversee set designs and costumes and decide where scenes should be shot, what backgrounds might be needed, and how special effects could be used. Directors might also book crew members, hire vendors, and ensure that gear and locations are secured. Music video producers may handle some of these tasks so that the director can focus on the more artistic aspects of the production.

Music video directors are occasionally assisted by *directors of photography* (DPs), or *cinematographers*, who are responsible for organizing and implementing the actual camera work. The director and the DP interpret scenes and decide on appropriate camera motion to achieve desired results. The DP determines the amounts of natural and artificial lighting required for each shoot and such technical factors as the type of film to be used, camera angles and distance, depth of field, and focus.

Music videos, like motion pictures, are usually filmed out of sequence, meaning that the ending might be shot first and scenes from the middle of the video might not be filmed until the end of production. Directors are responsible for scheduling each day's sequence of scenes. They coordinate filming so that scenes using the same set and performers will be filmed together. In addition to conferring with the producer and the DP (if one is used during the shoot), music video directors meet with technicians and crew members to advise on and approve final scenery, lighting, props, and other necessary equipment. They are also involved with final approval of costumes and choreography.

After all the scenes have been shot, postproduction begins. The director and producer work with *picture and sound editors* to cut apart and piece together the final product. The music video editor assembles shots according to the wishes of the director and producer and his or her own artistic sensibility, synchronizing film with voice and sound tracks produced by the sound editor and music editor.

When the music video is complete, the director and producer submit it to their employer (usually a record company or a production company) for final review. The employer may return the video for tweaking or major revisions. The video is revised and resubmitted until it meets the approval of the employer.

While music video directors and producers supervise all major aspects of music video production, various assistants—especially in big-budget productions—help throughout the process. In a less creative position than the director, the *first assistant director* organizes various practical matters involved during the shooting of each scene. The *second assistant director* is a coordinator who works as a liaison among the production office, the first assistant director, and the performers.

REQUIREMENTS

High School

The career paths of music video directors and producers are rather nontraditional. There is no standard training or normal progression up an industry ladder leading to the jobs of director or producer. At the very least, a high school diploma, while not technically required, will still probably be indispensable to you in terms of the background and education it signifies. (A high school diploma will be necessary if you decide to attend film school.) As is true of all artists, especially those in a medium as widely disseminated as music videos, you will need to have rich and varied experience in order to create works that are intelligently crafted and speak to people of many different backgrounds. In high school, courses in music, English (especially writing), art, theater, and history will give you a good foundation. If your high school offers film history or film production classes, be sure to take those courses. Visit the website of the American Film Institute (http://www.afi.edu) for a list of high schools that offer film courses and other resources for students and teachers. Take computer classes, since computer technology plays a major role in this industry. Finally, be active in school and community drama productions, whether as a performer, set designer, or cue-card holder.

High school courses that will be of assistance to you in your work as a producer include business, mathematics, English, speech, computer science, economics, music, and psychology.

Postsecondary Training
There are more than 500 film studies programs in the United States. According to the American Film Institute, the most reputable are Columbia University in New York City, New York University, the University of California at Los Angeles, and the University of Southern California.

The Music Video Commercial Institute (http://mvci.tv) in Los Angeles, California, is the only film school that specializes in training students to direct music video and commercial productions. Its six-month program, Directing for Music Videos and Commercials, consists of three sections: Introductory, Hands-On, and Workshop. The Introductory portion of the program focuses on the role of the director, basic cinematography and lighting, writing and pitching treatments, bidding, working with clients, production budgets, and legal issues. The Hands-On section covers topics such as editing, story and composition, advanced lighting techniques, basic compositing and postproduction, and working with and maintaining a camera. Workshop, the last program section, teaches how to plan a video shoot, storyboard projects, organize a production schedule and manage a budget, secure permits, and other topics. Students must complete and submit a final music video or commercial assignment as part of the program.

The debate continues on what is more influential in a music video directing career: personal experience or professional training. Some say that it is possible for creative people to land directing jobs without having gone through a formal program. Competition is so pervasive in the industry that even film school graduates find jobs scarce (only 5–10 percent of the 26,000 students who graduate from film schools each year find jobs in the industry). On the other hand, film school offers an education in fundamental directing skills by working with student productions. Such education is rigorous, but in addition to teaching skills it provides aspiring music video directors with peer groups and a network of contacts with students, faculty, and guest speakers that can be of help after graduation.

As with the career of director, a college degree is not required to be successful as a producer, but many producers earn college degrees. Formal study of business, film, television, music, communications, theater, writing, English literature, or art at the college level is helpful, as the music video producer must have a varied knowledge base to do his or her job successfully.

Other Requirements

Music video directors must have a strong creative vision for their projects, but they must be able to work with producers, editors, record company executives, and other industry professionals. They should be decisive leaders with an excellent knowledge of music videos and the narrative forms necessary to create them.

Music video producers come from a wide variety of backgrounds. Some start out as directors, musicians, business school graduates, actors, or production assistants. Many have never formally studied music video production or film. Most producers, however, get their positions through several years of experience in the industry, perseverance, and a keen sense for what projects will be artistically and commercially successful.

EXPLORING

To see if you have what it takes to be a music video director or producer, the most obvious opportunity for exploration lies in your own imagination. Studying music videos, films, and other types of media and the process of how they are made is the beginning of the journey to work in these fields.

In high school and beyond, pay attention to music videos. Watch them at every opportunity. Study commercials, television shows, and films that incorporate musical elements to see what makes them interesting. Try to imitate their style using your own or borrowed equipment—no matter how basic it is. Learn how to use a camera and how to edit what you shoot using a computer.

One of the best ways to get experience is to volunteer for a student or low-budget film project; positions on such projects are often advertised in local trade publications. Community cable stations also hire volunteers and may even offer internships.

You should also read trade journals such as *CVC Report* (http://www.cvcreport.com), an industry publication devoted to music video production and trends. To learn more about the music industry in general, read *Variety* (http://www.variety.com), *Rolling Stone* (http://www.rollingstone.com), and *Blender* (http://www.blender.com). The Directors Guild of America's official publication, *DGA Magazine,* contains much information on the industry. If you are unable to find this magazine at a public library or bookstore, visit the DGA website (http://www.dga.org) to read sample articles.

Many camps and workshops offer summer programs for high school students interested in film work. For example, UCLA offers its Media Workshops for students aged 14–24. Classes focus on mass media production, including film, TV, and video. For information, visit the Media Workshops Foundation website, http://www.mediaworkshops.org/foundation.

EMPLOYERS

Music video directors are usually employed on a freelance or contractual basis. Directors and producers find work, for example, with record companies, with advertising agencies, and through the creation of their own independent video projects. Keep in mind that the music video industry is not the only avenue for employment. Directors and producers work on documentaries, on television productions, in the film industry, and with various types of video presentations, from music to business. The greatest concentrations of music video directors and producers are in Los Angeles and New York City.

STARTING OUT

Rarely do people start their careers as music video directors or producers. With no set training methods, these jobs are hard to get just starting out. However, there are many things you can do to break into the industry.

First of all, you need to be willing to work for little or no money to get your foot in the door. To get started, ask local bands if you can

Notable Music Videos

1960s
"I Feel Fine" by The Beatles: Considered to be one of the first modern music videos

1970s
"Bohemian Rhapsody" by Queen: This long (nearly six minutes in length), sometimes bizarre video was nearly twice the length of a typical video.

"Rapper's Delight" by The Sugarhill Gang: The first rap video

1980s
"Video Killed the Radio Star" by The Buggles: The first video shown on MTV

"Union of the Snake" by Duran Duran: This was the first video released to MTV before its radio release.

"Thriller" by Michael Jackson: This 15-minute, special-effects-laden tour-de-force helped rewrite the rules for what a video could entail.

1990s
"Black or White" by Michael Jackson: Groundbreaking use of morphing technology

"Untitled (How Does It Feel)" by D'Angelo: More notorious than notable in that the entire video consisted of the musical artist singing naked.

2000s
"Star Guitar" by Chemical Brothers: Featured generous use of digital editing—a sign of innovations to come in the music video industry.

Source: http://www.nationmaster.com/encyclopedia/Music-video

direct their next video or see if you can do the same for your church choir or another local musical group. In short, grab any directing or producing opportunity that comes along, whether it relates to music or not.

Once you have gained some experience shooting or producing music videos, you should create a demo reel of your best work and send it to record companies and other potential employers. This will show employers that you are interested in and skilled enough to enter the industry.

Many in the industry suggest that aspiring directors and producers should try to land an internship or entry-level employment as a production assistant at a production company. In addition to your regular duties, you will learn how to bid on projects, get experience writing treatments, and learn production and business tips from directors and producers.

As mentioned earlier, film school is a great place to make contacts in the industry. Often, contacts are the essential factor in getting a job; many music video industry insiders agree that it's not only what you know but who you know that will get you a job. Networking often leads to good opportunities at various types of jobs in the industry. Many professionals recommend that those who want to become directors and producers should go to Los Angeles or New York, find any industry-related job, continue to take classes, and keep their eyes and ears open for news of job openings, especially with those professionals who are admired for their talent.

Another way to start out is through the Assistant Directors Training Program of the Directors Guild of America (address is listed at the end of this article). This program provides an excellent opportunity to those without industry connections to work on film and television productions. The program is based at two locations: New York City for the East Coast Program and Sherman Oaks, California, for the West Coast Program. Trainees receive hands-on experience through placement with major studios or on television movies and series. Programs also include formal training through mandatory seminars. The East Coast Program requires trainees to complete 350 days of on-set production work; the West Coast Program requires 400 days. While working, program trainees are paid a beginning weekly salary of $540. Once trainees have completed the program, they become freelance second assistant directors and can join the DGA. The competition is extremely stiff for these positions; each program usually accepts 20 or fewer trainees from among 800–1,200 applicants each year.

ADVANCEMENT

In the music video industry, advancement often comes with recognition. Directors who work on well-received music videos receive awards as well as more lucrative and prestigious job offers. Some directors choose to advance by leaving the music video industry for work in the motion picture or other related industries. Spike Jonze is an excellent example of a music video director who made the jump to feature film directing. In the early 1990s, Jonze made a name as the director of well-received music videos for REM and the Beastie Boys. He then used the skills he developed directing music videos to create award-winning feature films such as *Being John Malkovich* and *Adaptation*. Other music video directors who have made the transition to feature-film directing include Brett Ratner (*Rush Hour, Red Dragon*), David Fincher (*Fight Club, Panic Room*), and Michael Bay (*Armageddon, Pearl Harbor*).

Advancement for producers is generally measured by the types of projects they do, increased earnings, and respect in the field. Some producers become directors or make enough money to finance their own projects.

EARNINGS

According to the *Music Video Insider*, music video directors earn approximately 10 percent of a video's operating budget before production fees and insurance costs are factored into the budget. Budgets can range from as little as a few thousand dollars to millions of dollars for the creation of a video for a top artist. The U.S. Department of Labor reports that directors and producers earned salaries that ranged from less than $23,300 to $119,760 or more in 2002. The median annual salary for directors and producers employed in the video and motion picture industries was $75,440. Directors and producers who work on a freelance basis must pay for their own health insurance as well as the costs of operating a business.

WORK ENVIRONMENT

The work of the music video director can be glamorous and prestigious. But directors work under great stress, meeting deadlines, staying within budgets, and resolving problems among staff members. "Nine-to-five" definitely does not describe a day in the life of a music video director; 16-hour days (and more) are not uncommon. Because directors are ultimately responsible for every aspect of a video, schedules often dictate that they become immersed in their work around the clock, from preproduction to final cut. Nonetheless, those able to make it in the industry find their work to be extremely enjoyable and satisfying.

Music video producers have greater control over their working conditions than most other people working in the music video industry. They may have the autonomy of setting their own hours and delegating duties to others as necessary. The work often brings considerable personal satisfaction, but it is not without constraints. Producers must work within a stressful schedule complicated by competing work demands and daily crises. Long hours and weekend work are common.

Music video directors and producers frequently travel to meetings with potential employers and to filming locations. Music videos are made in almost every setting imaginable—from a dark, dingy warehouse to a Caribbean beach to a nondescript sidewalk in a small town. Successful directors and producers enjoy traveling and the demanding aspects of work in this field.

OUTLOOK

According to the U.S. Department of Labor, employment for directors and producers is expected to grow faster than the average for all occupations over the next several years. Though opportunities will increase with the expansion of cable and satellite television and an increased overseas demand for American-made music videos and films, competition is extreme and turnover is high. Most positions in the music video industry are held on a freelance basis. As is the case with most careers in the music video industry, directors and producers are usually hired to work on one video at a time. After a video is completed, new contacts must be made for further assignments.

FOR MORE INFORMATION

For information on the AFI Conservatory, AFI workshops, AFI awards, and other film and television news, contact
American Film Institute (AFI)
2021 North Western Avenue
Los Angeles, CA 90027
Tel: 323-856-7600
http://www.afi.com

For information on scholarships and publications, contact
Broadcast Education Association
1771 N Street, NW
Washington, DC 20036
Tel: 888-380-7222
http://www.beaweb.org

Visit the DGA website to read selections from DGA Magazine, *get industry news, and find links to film schools and film festivals.*
Directors Guild of America (DGA)
7920 Sunset Boulevard
Los Angeles, CA 90046
Tel: 310-289-2000
http://www.dga.org

For more information about the DGA's Assistant Directors Training Program, visit the following websites:
East Coast Program
http://www.dgatrainingprogram.org
West Coast Program
http://www.trainingplan.org

For information about a career as a producer in the motion picture and television industries, contact
Producers Guild of America
8530 Wilshire Boulevard, Suite 450
Beverly Hills, CA 90211
Tel: 310-358-9020
http://www.producersguild.org

Music Video Insider *is an e-zine for aspiring and professional music video directors. It offers message boards, FAQs, and articles about the music video industry.*
Music Video Insider
http://www.musicvideoinsider.com

Music Video Editors

QUICK FACTS

School Subjects
Art
Computer science
Music

Personal Skills
Artistic
Communication/ideas

Work Environment
Primarily indoors
Primarily one location

Minimum Education Level
Some postsecondary training

Salary Range
$20,030 to $38,270 to
$78,070+

Certification or Licensing
Voluntary

Outlook
Faster than the average

DOT
962

GOE
01.01.01

NOC
5131

O*NET-SOC
27-4032.00

OVERVIEW

Music video editors perform an essential role in the music industry: They take an unedited draft of film or videotape and use specialized equipment to improve the draft until it is ready for viewing. It is the responsibility of the video editor to create the most effective product possible that reflects the intentions of the featured music artist—or more precisely, the artist's record label.

HISTORY

The origins of the music video go deeper than the historic launch of MTV in 1981. Almost 100 years prior to that event, a photographer named George Thomas put together the first live-model illustrated song. Set to the song "The Little Lost Child," this series of photographic images hit vaudeville stages, and later, movie theaters. Customers lined up to see the shows. Suddenly, a new music sub-industry was born: illustrating popular songs to help sell musical numbers to the public—in this case, sheet music.

The first music videos were called Soundies, and were composed of footage of a band or a solo singer simply performing their song on a stage. These Soundies were used to promote artists as they are today. Nowadays, stylistic (and often provocative) music videos are made to sell albums and concert tickets.

Early video editing was sometimes done by the video's director, studio technicians, or other film staffers. Now, however, most full-length music videos have an editor who is responsible for the continuity and clarity of the project.

THE JOB

Music video editors work closely with video producers and directors throughout an entire project. These editors assist in the earliest phase, called preproduction, and during the production phase, when actual filming occurs. However, their skills are in the greatest demand during postproduction, when primary filming is completed and the bulk of the editing begins.

During preproduction, in meetings with producers and directors, video editors learn about the objectives of the music video. If the video is for a young pop star, for example, the editor should be familiar with his or her music and the image usually associated with the artist.

At this point, the producer may explain the larger scope of the project so that the editor knows the best way to approach the work when it is time to edit the film. In consultation with the director, editors may discuss the best way to accurately present the music artist's image. They may discuss different settings, scenes, costumes, special effects, or camera angles even before filming or taping begins. With this kind of preparation, music video editors are ready to practice their craft as soon as the production phase is complete.

Typically, the larger the budget for the video, the longer the shoot and the more time the editor will spend working in postproduction. Therefore, some editors may spend months on one project, while others may be working on several shorter projects simultaneously.

Editors first take film that has been developed in labs and transfer it to videotape. They then use digital editing systems to convert film footage to a digital format. The system has a database that tracks individual frames and puts all the scenes together in a folder of information. This information is stored on a hard drive and can instantly be brought up on screen, allowing a video editor to access scenes and frames with the click of a mouse.

Music video editors are usually the final decision makers when it comes to choosing which video segments will stay in as they are, which segments will be cut, or which may need to be redone. Editors look at the quality of the segment, its dramatic/entertainment value, and its relationship to the rest of the video. Editors then arrange the segments in an order that creates the most effective finished product. To do this, they rely on notes from the producer and director, along with their own natural sense of how scenes should look.

Some editors specialize in certain aspects of the music video. *Sound editors* may have training in music theory or performance and focus on the audio element of the music video. *Special effects editors* are

Best of 2003

According to MTV, these six music videos (in no particular order) were the best to come out in 2003:

- "Hey Ya" by OutKast
- "Go With the Flow" by Queens of the Stone Age
- "Stacy's Mom" by Fountains of Wayne
- "The Scientist" by Coldplay
- "Rock Your Body" by Justin Timberlake
- "Crazy in Love" by Beyoncé

Source: MTV.com

concerned more with the look of the video and are responsible for effects such as hand-drawn and computer animation and other stylistic footage.

REQUIREMENTS

High School

Because video editing requires a creative perspective along with technical skills, you should take English, speech, theater, and other courses that will allow you to develop writing skills. Art and photography classes will help you become more familiar with visual media. If you're lucky enough to attend a high school that offers classes in either film history or film production, be sure to take those courses. The American Film Institute hosts an educational website (http://www.afi.edu) that offers listings of high schools with film courses and other resources for teachers and students. Finally, don't forget to take computer classes. Editing work constantly makes use of new technology, and you should become familiar and comfortable with computers as soon as possible.

Postsecondary Training

While some employers may require a bachelor's degree for video editing work, actual on-the-job experience is the best guarantee of securing lasting employment. Degrees in liberal arts fields are preferred, but courses in cinematography and audiovisual techniques help editors get started in their work. You may choose to pursue a degree in such subjects as English, journalism, theater, or film. Community and two-year colleges often offer courses in the study of film history. Some of these colleges also teach film and video editing. Universities with departments of broadcast journalism offer courses in video editing and also may have contacts at local television stations.

Training as a music video editor takes from four to 10 years. Many editors learn much of their skills on the job as an assistant or apprentice at a film studio or production company. During an apprenticeship, the apprentice has the opportunity to see the work of the video editor up close. The editor may eventually assign some of his or her minor duties to the apprentice, while still making the larger decisions. After a few years the apprentice may be promoted to editor or may apply for a position at another studio or production company.

Certification or Licensing
Music video editors must be experts at using technology and software. Avid, Final Cut Pro, and other digital editing systems offer training and certification programs. Becoming certified is a good way for editors to increase their marketability. But, as everywhere in the arts, people get jobs through their talent, work, and contacts, not through certifications.

Other Requirements
To edit music videos, you should be able to work well with others and remain open to suggestions and guidance. A successful editor also has an understanding of the history and evolution of music videos and a feel for the narrative form in general. Computer skills are also important and will help you to learn new technology in the field.

EXPLORING

One of the best ways to prepare for a career as a music video editor is to stay current on music trends and new artists. You should also be familiar with all different kinds of film and television projects, including documentaries, short films, feature films, TV shows, and commercials. Study as many different projects as you can, paying close attention to the decisions the editors made in piecing together the scenes.

Large television stations and music production companies occasionally have volunteers or student interns. Most people in the industry start out doing minor tasks helping with production. These production assistants get the opportunity to see different professionals at work. By working closely with an editor, a production assistant can learn general video production operations as well as specific editing techniques.

EMPLOYERS

Some film or television editors work primarily with news programs, documentaries, or special features. They may develop ongoing working relationships with directors or producers who hire them from one project to another. Many editors who have worked for a studio or postproduction company for several years often become independent contractors. These editors offer their services on a per-job basis to producers of commercials and films, negotiate their own fees, and typically purchase or lease their own editing equipment.

STARTING OUT

Because of the glamour associated with television work, this is a popular field that can be very difficult to break into. With a minimum of a high school diploma or a degree from a two-year college, you can apply for entry-level jobs in many television studios and production companies, but these jobs won't be editing positions. Most employers will not consider you for an editor position if you don't have a bachelor's degree or several years of on-the-job experience.

One way to get on-the-job experience is to complete an apprenticeship in editing. However, in some cases you won't be eligible for an apprenticeship unless you are a current employee of the studio or production company. Therefore, start out by applying to as many studios as possible and take an entry-level position, even if it's not in the editing department. Once you start work, let people know that you are interested in an editor apprenticeship so that you'll be considered the next time a position becomes available.

Those who have completed bachelor's or master's degrees have typically gained hands-on experience through school projects. Another benefit of going to school is that contacts that you make while in school, both through your school's placement office and alumni, can be a valuable resource when you look for your first job. Your school's placement office may also have listings of job openings. Some studio work is union regulated. Therefore you may also want to contact union locals to find out about job requirements and openings.

ADVANCEMENT

Once video editors have secured employment in their field, their advancement comes with further experience and greater recognition. Some editors develop good working relationships with music video directors or producers. These editors may be willing to leave the security of a job at a production company for the possibility of working one-on-one with the director or producer on a project. These opportunities often provide editors with the autonomy they may not get in their regular jobs. Some are willing to take a pay cut to work on a video they feel is important.

Some video editors choose to stay at their production companies and advance through seniority to editing positions with higher salaries. They may be able to negotiate better benefits packages or to choose the projects they will work on. They may also choose which directors they wish to work with.

Some sound editors may wish to broaden their skills by working as general video editors. On the other hand, some general video editors may choose to specialize in sound effects, music, or some other editorial area. Some music video editors may move to television, motion pictures, or commercial work.

EARNINGS

Music video editors are not as highly paid as others working in their industry. They have less clout than directors or producers, but they have more authority in the production of a project than camera operators and technicians working on the set. According to the U.S. Department of Labor, the median annual wage for television and video editors was $38,270 in 2002. A small percentage of editors earned less than $20,030 a year, while some earned more than $78,070. The most experienced and sought-after video editors can command much higher salaries.

WORK ENVIRONMENT

Most video editors work in studios or at production companies. The working environment is often a small, cramped studio office full of editing equipment. Work hours vary widely depending on the scope of the video. Music videos are often filmed to be aired in conjunction with single and record release dates, so editors may be required to work overtime to meet deadlines.

During filming, video editors may be asked to be on hand at the filming location. Locations may be outdoors or in other cities, and travel is occasionally required. More often, however, the editor works in the studio.

Disadvantages of the job involve the video editor's low rank on the totem pole. However, most editors feel that this is outweighed by the honor of working on exciting projects.

OUTLOOK

The outlook for film, television, and video editors is very good. In fact, the U.S. Department of Labor predicts faster than average employment growth for video editors over the next several years. The growth in popularity of cable music channels will translate into greater demand for video editors. This will also force the largest production companies to offer more competitive salaries in order to attract the best editors.

The digital revolution is greatly affecting the editing process. Already, there are more than 20,000 Avid media systems (digital editing equipment) worldwide. Editors will work much more closely with special effects houses in putting together projects. When using more visual and sound effects, video editors will have to edit scenes with an eye toward the special effects that will be added. Digital editing systems are also available for home computers. Users can feed their own digital video into their computers, then edit the material, and add their own special effects and titles. This technology may allow some prospective editors more direct routes into the industry, but the majority of video editors will have to follow traditional routes, obtaining years of hands-on experience to advance in their careers.

FOR MORE INFORMATION

For information about AFI's Conservatory's master of fine arts in editing and to read interviews with professionals, visit the AFI website.

American Film Institute (AFI)
2021 North Western Avenue
Los Angeles, CA 90027
Tel: 323-856-7600
http://www.afi.com

This union counts film and television production workers among its craft members. For education and training information as well as links to film commissions and production companies, check out the IATSE website's Craft Page: Film and Television Production.

International Alliance of Theatrical Stage Employees, Moving Picture Technicians, Artists and Allied Crafts of the United States and Canada (IATSE)
1430 Broadway, 20th Floor
New York, NY 10018
Tel: 212-730-1770
http://www.iatse-intl.org

This organization offers training seminars and other resources to music video professionals.

Music Video Production Association
201 North Occidental Street
Building 7, Unit B
Los Angeles, CA 90026
Tel: 213-387-1590
http://www.mvpa.com

For information on NATAS scholarships and to read articles from Television Quarterly, the organization's official journal, visit the NATAS website.

National Academy of Television Arts and Sciences (NATAS)
111 West 57th Street, Suite 600
New York, NY 10019
Tel: 212-586-8424
http://www.emmyonline.org

Pop/Rock Musicians

QUICK FACTS

School Subjects
Business
Music

Personal Skills
Artistic
Communication/ideas

Work Environment
Indoors and outdoors
Primarily multiple locations

Minimum Education Level
High school diploma

Salary Range
$25 to $25,000 to
$1,000,000+

Certification or Licensing
None available

Outlook
About as fast as the average

DOT
152

GOE
01.04.04

NOC
5133

O*NET-SOC
27-2042.00, 27-2042.02

OVERVIEW

Pop/rock musicians perform in nightclubs, concert halls, on college campuses, and at live events such as festivals and fairs. They also record their music for distribution on CDs and audio cassettes. A pop/rock musician usually performs as a member of a band consisting of instrumentalists and vocalists. The band may perform original music or music composed and recorded by other artists or a combination of both.

HISTORY

Since the term "rock 'n' roll" was first coined by radio disc jockey Alan Freed in the 1950s, rock music has been a significant part of teenage culture. Rock music has always been marketed to teens, purchased by teens, and stirred controversy with parents. Though much of rock music has appealed to listeners of all ages, it was the teen culture that evolved in the 1950s that brought the doo-wop and boogie-woogie music of the South to audiences all across the country. Teens, for the first time in U.S. history, were spending their own money, and they were spending it on the records they heard on the radio. With the success of artists such as Chuck Berry, Little Richard, and Fats Domino; and later, Elvis Presley and Jerry Lee Lewis, music that had primarily been appreciated by black audiences was brought to a much wider market.

To capitalize on this popularity, recording companies hired songwriters, singers, and musicians to produce rock songs for the masses. Girl groups, such as the Ronettes, formed in the 1960s. Later that decade, rock took on more diverse sounds, as Motown artists, the Beatles, and other performers experimented with the genre. Though this experimentation led to a variety of musical forms in the 1970s, including folk, heavy metal, disco, and punk, record sales slipped, but not for long. The 1980s saw the rise in popularity of the music video and MTV, a cable network that brought music back to the teen culture and revived the music industry.

By the 1990s several networks had followed MTV's example, broadcasting music videos, concerts, and interviews with stars, along with other programming focused on music. And, as in the past, musical styles continued to develop. Grunge, a sound that drew on classic rock and punk music and included an attitude opposing mainstream culture, began with a number of bands mainly from the Seattle area. Nirvana and Pearl Jam eventually became two of the leading groups associated with grunge music that gained national and international popularity. Rap, a style of music in which rhyming lyrics are spoken over music, and hip hop, which includes saying lyrics over music and scratching records, also became nationally popular during this decade, although their roots can be traced back as far as the 1970s. Industrial, house, and techno music are other music styles that became widely popular in the 1990s and 2000s, but which began their development in earlier decades.

THE JOB

The lives and lifestyles of pop/rock stars—complete with limousines, groupies, and multimillion dollar record deals—are popular subjects for magazines, TV entertainment shows, and even movies. Though most pop/rock musicians do long for this kind of success, many have careers that are far less glamorous and financially rewarding than they appear. Nevertheless, for those who are devoted to their music, this work can be extremely fulfilling. Pop/rock musicians don't need to live in a major city, have international tours, or record top-selling CDs in order to enjoy this career. Opportunities for this work exist across the country. According to the Recording Workshop, a school for the recording arts in Ohio, most cities of over 25,000 have at least one audio production studio. These studios cater to the many rock musicians writing songs, performing them, and promoting their music to regional and national audiences. Typically, pop/rock musicians have an interest in music while they are still young. They may learn to play an instrument, to sing, or to write music, and they begin to perform publicly, even if it's just for the neighborhood block party. Over time, with increasing skills and contacts in the field, they develop lives that involve performing music on a regular basis.

Julia Greenberg is a rock musician in New York who has devoted years to the pursuit of a career in the music industry. Her first CD, *Past Your Eyes,* received glowing reviews from the *New York Times, CMJ New Music Report, Performing Songwriter,* and the *Village Voice.* Greenberg has worked very hard for many years to reach her current level of success. "I started my own band, using all original music, in 1993," she says. "I hired musicians and old friends to arrange the songs to play on my first demo. I used the demo to get gigs at clubs." Her band was very well received, and she has managed to get gigs all around Manhattan ever since. She's played at clubs, such as Mercury Lounge, Fez, and Brownie's, that are famous for promoting new and established acts. "My music is in the singer/songwriter vein," she says. "I'm very much focused on the writing. But we're also a straight-ahead rock band." Her work is influenced by classic rock and music by acts such as Blondie and Elvis Costello, with which she grew up.

In order to be truly successful, pop/rock musicians need original material to perform. Some regional bands, however, do make careers for themselves by playing the music of famous bands, performing at local clubs, dances, wedding receptions, and private parties. They may specialize in a specific period of music, such as music of the 1980s or Motown hits of the 1960s. But A&R (artist and repertoire) coordinators for record companies, managers, producers, and other professionals in the recording industry are looking for musicians who write and perform their own music.

Pop/rock musicians must spend much time practicing their skills away from the stage. They work on writing music and lyrics, practicing their instruments, and practicing together as a band. Rehearsal time and commitment to the band are extremely important to these musicians. In order for the band to sound as good as it possibly can, all the instrumentalists and vocalists must develop a sense of each other's talents and styles. In order to promote their band, the members put together a tape (called a *demo*) demonstrating their work and talent, which they then submit to club managers and music producers. When making a demo or recording a CD for a record company, bands record in studios and work with recording professionals. Audio engineers, producers, and mixing engineers help to enhance the band's performance in order to make their music sound as good as it possibly can.

When booked by a club, the club's promotional staff may advertise a band's upcoming appearance. For the most part, however, bands that are not well known must do their own advertising. This can involve distributing flyers, sending press releases to area newspapers and arts weeklies, and sending announcements to those on

Pop/rock musicians frequently perform live to attract new fans.
(Jim Whitmer Photography)

their mailing list. A band's mailing list is composed of the names and addresses of people who have attended previous performances and have expressed interest in hearing about future gigs. Many bands also maintain websites listing their performance schedule. Of course, very successful pop/rock musicians have an established fan base, and their record company or promoter handles all the advertising.

On the day of the performance, pop/rock groups arrive early to prepare the stage for their show. This involves setting up instruments and sound systems, checking for sound quality, and becoming familiar with the stage and facility. Together, the band goes over the list of songs to be performed.

The size, mood, and age of the audience will likely affect a group's performance. If they are playing to a small crowd in a club, they will probably have much more personal experiences (as they see individual audience members and gauge their reactions to songs) than when playing to an auditorium full of hundreds of people. If the audience is enthusiastic about the music, instead of simply waiting for the next band scheduled to appear, the musicians are likely to have a positive experience and perform well. Age of audience members is also a factor, because older crowds may have the opportunity to drink alcohol, which may make them less inhibited about being loud and showing their pleasure or displeasure over a performance. Regardless of the audience, however, professional musicians play each song to the best of their abilities, with the intention of entertaining and enlightening listeners and developing a strong base of devoted fans.

REQUIREMENTS

High School
High school classes that will help you become a pop/rock musician include English, which will help you hone your writing abilities; business and mathematics, which will teach you basic business principles of budgeting and managing money; and, of course, music, specifically voice or instrument training. Playing in one or more of your high school bands will give you an idea of what it is like to interact with fellow musicians as well as perform in front of an audience.

Postsecondary Training
A college education isn't necessary for becoming a pop/rock musician, but it can help you learn about music, recording, and writing. In general, you should have a background in music theory and an understanding of a variety of styles of music. Learning to play one or more instruments, such as the piano or guitar, will be especially helpful in writing songs. You can pursue this education at a community college, university, or trade school. There are a number of seminars, conferences, and workshops available that will involve you with songwriting, audio recording, and producing.

Other Requirements
You need to be able to work closely with other artists and to have patience with the rehearsal and recording process. You'll also need persistence to proceed with your ambitions in the face of much rejection. "You have to have a really strong personality," Julia Greenberg says. "You have to be able to get up on stage and command a room. You have to be really starved for attention!"

EXPLORING

Talk to your music teachers at school about opportunities in music. Try to attend as many musical performances as possible; they don't all have to be in the pop/rock genre. Many clubs and other concert facilities offer all-ages shows where you can see musical artists perform firsthand. Depending on the size of the venue, you may have a chance to approach a musician after the show to ask a few questions about the field.

The best way to get experience is to learn to play an instrument or take voice lessons. Once you've mastered the basics, you can get together with friends or classmates and experiment with different musical styles. Don't forget the writing aspect of pop/rock music. Keep a journal of your thoughts and ideas. Read the lyrics of your favorite songs and try to figure out what makes them so appealing. Try to create the lyrics to a song of your own by combining this knowledge with your journal entries or other creative writing.

EMPLOYERS

Some pop/rock musicians work for another member of the band who pays them to rehearse and perform. But in most cases, pop/rock musicians work on a freelance basis, taking on gigs as they come. Bands are hired to play at clubs, concert halls, and for community events. They may also play private gigs, weddings, and other celebrations. Many musicians also maintain flexible day jobs that help to support them as they perform on the evenings and weekends.

STARTING OUT

Many bands form when a group of friends get together to collaborate on the writing and performing of original songs. However, openings for band members are frequently advertised in the classifieds of local and college newspapers and arts weeklies. You may have to audition for many bands before you find one with which you fit, or you may have to put together your own group of musicians. If part of a new band, you'll have to put a lot of time into rehearsal, as well as gaining a following. This may involve playing a lot of shows for free until a club owner can rely on you to bring in a crowd.

ADVANCEMENT

The sky's the limit when it comes to advancing in the music industry. Once musicians have made the right connections, they may find themselves with record deals, national concert dates, awards, and a great deal of media attention. Julia Greenberg dreams of success that will allow her to perform and write music full time. Through the help of independent investors, Greenberg has been able to finance a new demo. "I'm shopping the CD to industry people, and putting the CD out myself," she says. "A lot of people are doing this these days. Industry people are looking for artists who can get their own following."

EARNINGS

Even professionals with regular club dates have difficulty predicting how much money they will earn from one year to the next. And for those just starting out, many will earn nothing as they play clubs and events for free in order to establish themselves on the music scene. Their goal may be simply to get paying shows where they can earn enough money to cover their expenses (for example, for travel and promotion). As groups become better known and can be relied on to draw an audience, they may be paid a percentage of a club's cover charge or drink receipts.

When playing for special occasions such as weddings, birthday parties, and bar mitzvahs, pop/rock groups can earn anything from a token amount, such as $25, to $1,000 or more once they have become well known in an area. While $1,000 might sound like a lot of money for a few hours of stage work, in reality the sum each musician gets will be much less. For example, if there are four members in the group, each will only receive $250—but this is before expenses and taxes. Once these have been figured in, each member may end up making less than $200. Now assume these musicians have fairly steady work and perform once almost every week for the year. At that rate, they would each be earning approximately $9,000 to $10,000 annually. Obviously this is not enough to live on, which is why so many musicians work at a second job.

Musicians who are able to come up with the right sound and make the right contacts in the industry may begin touring on a national level, increase their fan base, and sell recordings of their music. Those who are able to do this on a steady basis may have earnings in the $20,000–$30,000 range. At the very top of the business, a few groups have earnings into the millions for one year. Even then, however, this money must be divided among the group members, backup singers, agents, and others.

Most pop/rock musicians are freelancers, moving from one performance to the next and getting paid by various clients. Because of this, they have no employer that provides benefits such as health insurance and paid vacation time. Therefore these musicians must provide their own benefits.

WORK ENVIRONMENT

Creative people can be a temperamental bunch, and some musicians can be difficult to get along with. Working closely with such people can at times create a tense or unpleasant environment. On the other hand, the opportunity to perform with talented musicians can be inspiring and offer opportunities to learn new things about music. Rehearsing requires a great deal of time and late hours, but can result in excellent work. Pop/rock musicians may perform in dark, smoky bars, in large hotel dining rooms, or in open-air auditoriums. They must be prepared to work in a variety of settings, some of which may not have the best acoustics or the proper amount of space for all the instruments and band members. The professional musician learns to adapt to the performance area, making adjustments with sound systems, the music to be played, or even the instruments used. Travel is a part of this work. Even those musicians who only perform in one or two towns must get to and from different performance sites with their equipment in order to work. And any pop or rock musician who wants to advance his or her career should be prepared to be on the road a great deal of the time.

OUTLOOK

There will always be thousands more pop/rock musicians than there are record contracts. But there will also always be opportunities for new performers with record companies and clubs. Record companies are always on the lookout for original sounds and talents. Even with a record deal, however, there are no guarantees of success. The music industry, and the CD-buying public, have fickle tastes. Often rock musicians are dropped by their label when record sales fail to meet expectations.

With recording studios becoming more sophisticated, artists can more effectively promote themselves with quality CDs. Record companies will be paying close attention to these independently produced CDs when scouting for new talent.

FOR MORE INFORMATION

For information on membership in a local union nearest you, developments in the music field, a searchable database of U.S. and foreign music schools, and articles on careers in music, visit the following website.

American Federation of Musicians of the United States and Canada
1501 Broadway, Suite 600
New York, NY 10036
Tel: 212-869-1330
http://www.afm.org

The AGMA is a union for professional musicians. The website has information on upcoming auditions, news announcements for the field, and membership information.
American Guild of Musical Artists (AGMA)
1430 Broadway, 14th Floor
New York, NY 10018
Tel: 212-265-3687
http://www.musicalartists.org

For information about the music field as well as career development opportunities, such as songwriting workshops for the pop music composer, contact
American Society of Composers, Authors, and Publishers
One Lincoln Plaza
New York, NY 10023
Tel: 212-621-6000
http://www.ascap.com

GigAmerica is a useful fee-based service for up-and-coming musicians. It provides assistance with marketing, tour development, CD duplication, and other aspects of developing a successful music career.
GigAmerica
1123 Broadway, Suite 317
New York, NY 10010
Tel: 212-367-0826
http://www.gigamerica.com

The SGA offers song critiques and other workshops in select cities. Visit its website for further information on such events.
Songwriters Guild of America (SGA)
1500 Harbor Boulevard
Weehawken, NJ 07086
Tel: 201-867-7603
http://www.songwriters.org

Singers

OVERVIEW

Professional *singers* perform opera, gospel, blues, rock, jazz, folk, classical, country, and other musical genres before an audience or in recordings. Singers are musicians who use their voices as their instruments. They may perform as part of a band, choir, or other musical ensemble, or solo, whether with or without musical accompaniment. Singers, musicians, and related workers hold approximately 240,000 jobs in the United States.

HISTORY

"Song is man's sweetest joy," said a poet in the eighth century B.C. Singers are people who use their voices as instruments and are capable of relating music that elicits a variety of emotions. The verb to sing is related to the Greek term *omphe*, which means voice. In general, singing is related to music and thus to the muses, the goddesses of ancient Greek religion who are said to watch over the arts and are sources of inspiration.

Singing, or vocal performance, is considered the mother of all music, which is thought of as an international language. In human history, before musical instruments were ever devised, there was always the voice, which has had the longest and most significant influence on the development of all musical forms and materials that have followed.

Singing evolved in different parts of the world and in diverse ways at various times. A 40,000-year-old cave painting in France suggests the earliest evidence of music; the painting shows a man playing a musical bow and dancing behind several reindeer. Most civilizations have had legends suggesting that gods created song, and many myths suggest that nymphs have passed the art of singing to us. The Chinese

QUICK FACTS

School Subjects
Music
Speech

Personal Skills
Artistic
Communication/ideas

Work Environment
Primarily indoors
Primarily multiple locations

Minimum Education Level
High school diploma

Salary Range
$13,040 to $36,290 to $96,250+

Certification or Licensing
None available

Outlook
About as fast as the average

DOT
152

GOE
01.04.03

NOC
5133

O*NET-SOC
27-2042.00, 27-2042.01

philosopher Confucius considered music to be a significant aspect of a moral society, with its ability to portray emotions as diverse as joy and sorrow, anger and love.

There are certain differences between Eastern and Western music. In general, music of Middle Eastern civilizations has tended to be more complex in its melodies (although music from the Far East is often simplistic). Western music has been greatly influenced by the organized systems of musical scales of ancient Greece and has evolved through various eras, which were rich and enduring but can be defined in general terms. The first Western musical era is considered to have been the medieval period (c. 850–1450), when the earliest surviving songs were written by 12th-century French troubadours and German minnesingers; these poet-musicians sang of love, nature, and religion. The next periods include the Renaissance (c. 1450–1600), during which the musical attitude was one of calm and self-restraint; the baroque period (c. 1600–1750), a time of extravagance, excitement, and splendor; the classical period (c. 1750–1820), a return to simplicity; and the Romantic period (c. 1820–1950), which represents a time of strong emotional expression and fascination with nature.

In primitive societies of the past and present, music has played more of a ritualistic, sacred role. In any case, singing has been considered an art form for thousands of years, powerfully influencing the evolution of societies. It is a large part of our leisure environment, our ceremonies, and our religions; the power of song has even been said to heal illness and sorrow. In antiquity, musicians tended to have more than one role, serving as composer, singer, and instrumentalist at the same time. They also tended to be found in the highest levels of society and to take part in events such as royal ceremonies, funerals, and processions.

The function of singing as an interpretive, entertaining activity was established relatively recently. Opera had its beginnings in the late 16th century in Italy and matured during the following centuries in other European countries. The rise of the professional singer (also referred to as the vocal virtuoso because of the expert talent involved) occurred in the 17th and 18th centuries. At this time, musical composers began to sing to wider audiences, who called for further expression and passion in singing.

Throughout the periods of Western music, the various aspects of song have changed along with general musical developments. Such aspects include melody, harmony, rhythm, tempo, dynamics, texture, and other characteristics. The structures of song are seemingly unlimited and have evolved from plainsong and madrigal, chanson and chorale, opera and cantata, folk and motet, anthem and drama, to today's expanse of pop, rock, country, rap, and so on. The development of radio, television, motion pictures, and various types of recordings (LP records, cassettes, compact discs, and digital audio) has had a great effect on the singing profession, creating smaller audiences for live performances yet larger and larger audiences for recorded music.

THE JOB

Essentially, singers are employed to perform music with their voices by using their knowledge of vocal sound and delivery, harmony, melody, and rhythm. They put their individual vocal styles into the songs they sing, and they interpret music accordingly. The inherent sounds of the voices in a performance play a significant part in how a song will affect an audience; this aspect of a singer's voice is known as *tone*.

Classical singers are usually categorized according to the range and quality of their voices, beginning with the highest singing voice, the soprano, and ending with the lowest, the bass; voices in between include mezzo soprano, contralto, tenor, and baritone. Singers perform either alone (in which case they are referred to as soloists) or as members of an ensemble, or group. They sing by either following a score, which is the printed musical text, or by memorizing the material. Also, they may sing either with or without instrumental accompaniment; singing without accompaniment is called *a cappella*. In opera—actually plays set to music—singers perform the various roles, much like actors, interpreting the drama with their voices to the accompaniment of a symphony orchestra.

Classical singers may perform a variety of musical styles, or specialize in a specific period; they may give recitals, or perform as members of an ensemble. Classical singers generally undergo years of voice training and instruction in musical theory. They develop their vocal technique and learn how to project without harming their voices. Classical singers rarely use a microphone when they sing; nonetheless, their voices must be heard above the orchestra. Because classical singers often perform music from many different languages, they learn how to pronounce these languages, and often how to speak them as well. Those who are involved in opera work for opera companies in major cities throughout the country and often travel extensively. Some classical singers also perform in other musical areas.

Professional singers tend to perform in a certain chosen style of music, such as jazz, rock, or blues, among many others. Many singers pursue careers that will lead them to perform for coveted recording contracts, on concert tours, and for television and motion pictures. Others perform in rock, pop, country, gospel, or folk groups, singing in concert halls, nightclubs, churches, and at social gatherings and for small studio recordings. Whereas virtuosos (classical artists who are expertly skilled in their singing style) tend to perform traditional pieces that have been handed down through hundreds of years, singers in other areas often perform popular, current pieces, and often songs that they themselves have composed.

Another style of music in which formal training is often helpful is jazz. *Jazz singers* learn phrasing, breathing, and vocal techniques; often, the goal of a jazz singer is to become as much a part of the instrumentation as the piano, saxophone, trumpet, or trombone. Many jazz singers perform "scat" singing, in which the voice is used in an improvisational way much like any other instrument.

Folk singers perform songs that may be many years old, or they may write their own songs. Folk singers generally perform songs that express a certain cultural tradition; while some folk singers specialize in their own or another culture, others may sing songs from a great variety of cultural and musical traditions. In the United States, folk singing is particularly linked to the acoustic guitar, and many singers accompany themselves while singing.

A cappella singing, which is singing without musical accompaniment, takes many forms. A cappella music may be a part of classical music; it may also be a part of folk music, as in the singing of barbershop quartets. Another form, called doo-wop, is closely linked to rock and rhythm and blues music.

Gospel music, which evolved in the United States, is a form of sacred music; *gospel singers* generally sing as part of a choir, accompanied by an organ, or other musical instruments, but may also perform a cappella. Many popular singers began their careers as singers in church and gospel choirs before entering jazz, pop, blues, or rock.

Pop/rock singers generally require no formal training whatsoever. Rock music is a very broad term encompassing many different styles of music, such as heavy metal, punk, rap, rhythm and blues, rockabilly, techno, and many others. Many popular rock singers cannot even sing. But rock singers learn to express themselves and their music, developing their own phrasing and vocal techniques. Rock singers usually sing as part of a band, or with a backing band to accompany them. Rock singers usually sing with microphones so that they can be heard above the amplified instruments around them.

All singers practice and rehearse their songs and music. Some singers read from music scores while performing; others perform from memory. Yet all must gain an intimate knowledge of their music, so that they can best convey its meanings and feelings to their audience. Singers must also exercise their voices even when not performing. Some singers perform as featured soloists and artists. Others perform as part of a choir, or as backup singers adding harmony to the lead singer's voice.

REQUIREMENTS

High School

Many singers require no formal training in order to sing. However, those interested in becoming classical or jazz singers should begin learning and honing their talent when they are quite young. Vocal talent can be recognized in grade school students and even in younger children. In general, however, these early years are a time of vast development and growth in singing ability. Evident changes occur in boys' and girls' voices when they are around 12–14 years old, during which time their vocal cords go through a process of lengthening and thickening. Boys' voices tend to change much more so than girls' voices, although both genders should be provided with challenges that will help them achieve their talent goals. Young students should learn about breath control and why it is necessary; they should learn to follow a conductor, including the relationship between hand and baton motions and the dynamics of the music; and they should learn about musical concepts such as tone, melody, harmony, and rhythm.

During the last two years of high school, aspiring singers should have a good idea of what classification they are in, according to the range and quality of their voices: soprano, alto, contralto, tenor, baritone, or bass. These categories indicate the resonance of the voice (soprano being the highest and lightest, bass being the lowest and heaviest). Students should take part in voice classes, choirs, and ensembles. In addition, students should continue their studies in English, writing, social studies, foreign language, and other electives in music, theory, and performance.

There tend to be no formal educational requirements for those who wish to be singers. However, formal education is valuable, especially in younger years. Some students know early in their lives that they want to be singers and are ambitious enough to continue to practice and learn. These students are often advised to attend high schools that are specifically geared toward combined academic and intensive arts education in music, dance, and theater. Such schools can provide valuable preparation and guidance for those who plan to pursue professional careers in the arts. Admission is usually based on results from students' auditions as well as academic testing.

Postsecondary Training

Many find it worthwhile and fascinating to continue their study of music and voice in a liberal arts program at a college or university. Similarly, others attend schools of higher education that are focused specifically on music, such as the Juilliard School (http://www.juilliard.edu) in New York. Such an intense program would include a multidisciplinary curriculum of composition and performance, as well as study and appreciation of the history, development, and variety of and potential advances in music. In this type of program, a student would earn a bachelor of arts degree. To earn a bachelor of science degree in music, one would study musicology, which concerns the history, literature, and cultural background of music; the music industry, which will prepare one for not only singing but also marketing music and other business aspects; and professional performance. Specific music classes in a typical four-year liberal arts program would include such courses as introduction to music, music styles and structures, harmony, theory of music, elementary and advanced auditory training, music history, and individual instruction.

In addition to learning at schools, many singers are taught by *private singing teachers and voice coaches,* who help to develop and refine students' voices. Many aspiring singers take courses at continuing adult education centers, where they can take advantage of courses in beginning and advanced singing, basic vocal techniques, voice coaching, and vocal performance workshops. When one is involved in voice training, he or she must learn about good articulation and breath control, which are very important qualities for all singers. Performers must take care of their voices and keep their lungs in good condition. Voice training, whether as part of a college curriculum or in private study, is useful to many singers, not only for classical and opera singers, but also for jazz singers and for those interested in careers in musical theater. Many professional singers who have already "made it" continue to take voice lessons throughout their careers.

Other Requirements

In other areas of music, learning to sing and becoming a singer is often a matter of desire, practice, and an inborn love and talent for singing. Learning to play a musical instrument is often extremely helpful in learning to sing and to read and write music. Sometimes it is not even necessary to have a good singing voice. Many singers in rock music have less-than-perfect voices, and rap artists do not really sing at all. But these singers learn to use their voices in ways that nonetheless provide good expression to their songs, music, and ideas.

EXPLORING

Anyone who is interested in pursuing a career as a singer should obviously have a love for music. Listen to recordings as often as possible, and get an understanding of the types of music that you enjoy. Singing alone or with family and friends is one of the most natural ways to explore music and develop a sense of your own vocal style. Join music clubs at school, as well as the school band if it does vocal performances. In addition, take part in school drama productions that involve musical numbers.

Older students interested in classical music careers could contact trade associations such as the American Guild of Musical Artists, as well as read trade journals such as *Hot Line News* (published by Musicians National Hot Line Association), which covers news about singers and other types of musicians and their employment needs and opportunities. For information and news about very popular singers, read *Billboard* magazine (http://www.billboard.com), which can be purchased at many local bookshops and newsstands. Those who already know what type of music they wish to sing should audition for roles in community musical productions or contact trade groups that offer competitions. For example, the Central Opera Service (Metropolitan Opera, Lincoln Center, New York, NY 10023) can provide information on competitions, apprentice programs, and performances for young singers interested in opera.

There are many summer programs offered throughout the United States for high school students interested in singing and other performing arts. (See the end of this article for contact information on these programs.) For example, Stanford University offers its Stanford Jazz Workshop each summer for students who are at least 12 years old. It offers activities in instrumental and vocal music, as well as recreation in swimming, tennis, and volleyball. For college students who are 18 years and older, the jazz workshop has a number of job positions available.

Another educational institute that presents a summer program is Boston University's Tanglewood Institute, which is geared especially toward very talented and ambitious students between the ages of 15 and 18. It offers sessions in chorus, musical productions, chamber music, classical music, ensemble, instrumental, and vocal practice. Arts and culture field trips are also planned. College students who are at least 20 years old can apply for available jobs at the summer Tanglewood programs.

Students interested in other areas of singing can begin while still in high school, or even sooner. Many gospel singers, for example, start singing with their local church group at an early age. Many high school students form their own bands, playing rock, country, or jazz, and can gain experience performing before an audience; some of these young musicians even get paid to perform at school parties and other social functions.

EMPLOYERS

There are many different environments in which singers can be employed, including local lounges, bars, cafes, radio and television, theater productions, cruise ships, resorts, hotels, casinos, large concert tours, and opera companies.

Many singers hire agents, who usually receive a percentage of the singer's earnings for finding them appropriate performance contracts. Others are employed primarily as *studio singers,* which means that they do not perform for live audiences but rather record their singing in studios for albums, radio, television, and motion pictures.

An important tactic for finding employment as a singer is to invest in a professional-quality tape recording of your singing that you can send to prospective employers.

STARTING OUT

There is no single correct way of entering the singing profession. It is recommended that aspiring singers explore the avenues that interest them, continuing to apply and audition for whatever medium suits them. Singing is an extremely creative profession, and singers must learn to be creative and resourceful in the business matters of finding gigs.

High school students should seek out any opportunities to perform, including choirs, school musical productions, and church and other religious functions. Singing teachers can arrange recitals and introduce students to their network of musician contacts.

ADVANCEMENT

In the singing profession and the music industry in general, the nature of the business is such that singers can consider themselves to have "made it" when they get steady, full-time work. A measure of advancement is how well known and respected singers become in their field, which in turn influences their earnings. In most areas, particularly classical music, only the most talented and persistent singers make it to the top of their profession. In other areas, success may be largely a matter of luck and perseverance. A singer on Broadway, for example, may begin as a member of the chorus, and eventually become a featured singer. On the other hand, those who have a certain passion for their work and accept their career position tend to enjoy working in local performance centers, nightclubs, and other musical environments.

Also, many experienced singers who have had formal training will become voice teachers. Reputable schools such as Juilliard consider it a plus when a student can say that he or she has studied with a master.

EARNINGS

As with many occupations in the performing arts, earnings for singers are highly dependent on one's professional reputation and thus cover a wide range. To some degree, pay is also related to educational background (as it relates to how well one has been trained) and geographic location of performances. In certain situations, such as singing for audio recordings, pay is dependent on the number of minutes of finished music (for instance, an hour's pay will be given for each three and a half minutes of recorded song).

Singing is often considered a glamorous occupation. However, because it attracts so many professionals, competition for positions is very high. Only a small proportion of those who aspire to be singers achieve glamorous jobs and extremely lucrative contracts. Famous opera singers, for example, earn $8,000 and more for each performance. Singers in an opera chorus earn between $600 and $800 per week. Classical soloists can receive between $2,000 and $3,000 per performance, while choristers may receive around $70 per performance. For rock singers, earnings can be far higher. Within the overall group of professional singers, studio and opera singers tend to earn salaries that are well respected in the industry; their opportunities for steady, long-term contracts tend to be better than for singers in other areas.

Average salaries for musicians, singers, and related workers were $36,290 in 2002, according to the U.S. Department of Labor. The lowest paid 10 percent earned less than $13,040 per year, while the highest paid 10 percent earned more than $96,250 annually.

Top studio and opera singers earn an average of $70,000 per year, though some earn much more. Rock singers may begin by playing for drinks and meals only; if successful, they may earn tens of thousands of dollars for a single performance. Singers on cruise ships generally earn between $750 and $2,000 per week, although these figures can vary considerably. Also, many singers supplement their performance

To be successful live performers, singers need a distinctive vocal style and a strong stage presence. *(Jim Whitmer Photography)*

earnings by working at other positions, such as teaching at schools or giving private lessons or even working at jobs unrelated to singing. The U.S. Department of Labor reports that median salaries in 2002 for full-time teachers were as follows: elementary, $41,780; middle school, $41,820; and high school, $43,950. Full-time college professors earned an average of $60,000 in 2000–01, according to the American Association of University Professors.

Because singers rarely work for a single employer, they generally receive no fringe benefits and must provide their own health insurance and retirement planning.

WORK ENVIRONMENT

The environments in which singers work tend to vary greatly, depending on such factors as type of music involved and location of performance area. Professional singers often work in the evenings and during weekends, and many are frequently required to travel. Many singers who are involved in popular productions such as in opera, rock, and country music work in large cities such as New York, Las Vegas, Chicago, Los Angeles, and Nashville. Stamina and endurance are needed to keep up with the hours of rehearsals and performances, which can be long; work schedules are very often erratic, varying from job to job.

Many singers are members of trade unions, which represent them in matters such as wage scales and fair working conditions. Vocal performers who sing for studio recordings are represented by the American Federation of Television and Radio Artists; solo opera singers, solo concert singers, and choral singers are members of the American Guild of Musical Artists.

OUTLOOK

Any employment forecast for singers will most probably emphasize one factor that plays an important role in the availability of jobs: competition. Because so many people pursue musical careers and because there tend to be no formal requirements for employment in this industry (the main qualification is talent), competition is most often very strong.

According to the U.S. Department of Labor, employment for singers, as for musicians in general, is expected to grow about as fast as the average for all other occupations over the next several years. The entertainment industry is expected to grow during the next decade, which will create jobs for singers and other performers. Because of the nature of this work, positions tend to be temporary and part time; in fact, of all members of the American Federation of Musicians, fewer than 2 percent work full time in their singing careers. Thus, it is often advised that those who are intent on pursuing a singing career keep in mind the varied fields other than performance in which their interest in music can be beneficial, such as composition, education, broadcasting, therapy, and community arts management.

Those intent on pursuing singing careers in rock, jazz, and other popular forms should understand the keen competition they will face. There are thousands of singers all hoping to make it; only a very few actually succeed. However, there are many opportunities to perform in local cities and communities, and those with a genuine love of singing and performing should also possess a strong sense of commitment and dedication to their art.

FOR MORE INFORMATION

For information on membership in a local union nearest you, developments in the music field, a searchable database of U.S. and foreign music schools, and articles on careers in music, visit the following website:

American Federation of Musicians of the United States and Canada
1501 Broadway, Suite 600
New York, NY 10036
Tel: 212-869-1330
http://www.afm.org

For information on union membership, contact
American Federation of Television and Radio Artists
260 Madison Avenue
New York, NY 10016-2401
Tel: 212-532-0800
http://www.aftra.com

The AGMA is a union for professional musicians. The website has information on upcoming auditions, news announcements for the field, and membership information.
American Guild of Musical Artists (AGMA)
1430 Broadway, 14th Floor
New York, NY 10018
Tel: 212-265-3687
Email: AGMA@MusicalArtists.org
http://www.musicalartists.org

For more information on Hot Line News, *contact*
Musicians National Hot Line Association
277 East 6100 South

Salt Lake City, UT 84107
Tel: 801-268-2000

For a list of colleges and universities that offer music-related programs, contact
National Association of Schools of Music
11250 Roger Bacon Drive, Suite 21
Reston, VA 20190
Tel: 703-437-0700
http://nasm.arts-accredit.org

For career and educational information for opera singers, contact
Opera America
1156 15th Street, Suite 810
Washington, DC 20005
Tel: 202-293-4466
http://www.operaam.org

For information on music programs, contact the following:
Boston University, Tanglewood Institute
855 Commonwealth Avenue
Boston, MA 02215
http://www.bu.edu/cfa/music/tanglewood

Stanford University, Jazz Workshop
Box 20454
Stanford, CA 94309
Tel: 650-736-0324
http://www.stanfordjazz.org

Songwriters

QUICK FACTS

School Subjects
English
Music

Personal Skills
Artistic
Communication/ideas

Work Environment
Primarily indoors
Primarily one location

Minimum Education Level
High school diploma

Salary Range
$20,000 to $50,000 to
$1,000,000+

Certification or Licensing
None available

Outlook
About as fast as the average

DOT
131

GOE
01.01.02

NOC
5132

O*NET-SOC
27-2041.02, 27-2041.03

OVERVIEW

Songwriters write the words and music for songs, including songs for recordings, advertising jingles, and theatrical performances. We hear the work of songwriters every day, and yet most songwriters remain anonymous, even if a song's performer is famous. Many songwriters perform their own songs.

HISTORY

Songwriting played an important part in the growth of the United States. The early pioneers wrote songs as a way to relax. Some of the difficult experiences of traveling, fighting over land, farming, and hunting for food were put into words by early songwriters, and the words set to music, for the guitar, banjo, piano, and other instruments. Francis Scott Key became famous for writing the words to the "Star Spangled Banner," set to a popular drinking tune.

Toward the end of the 19th century, sheet music was sold by dozens and even hundreds of publishing companies, centered in New York City in what became known as Tin Pan Alley. Songwriter Monroe Rosenfeld coined this name. It referred to the sounds of many voices and pianos coming from the open windows of the street where many of the music publishers were located. By the 1880s, sheet music sold by the millions; most songs were introduced on the stages of musical theater, vaudeville, and burlesque shows. Radio became an important medium for introducing new songs in the 1920s, followed by the introduction of sound movies in the 1930s. Sheet music became less important as musical recordings were introduced. This presented difficulties for the songwriter and publisher, because the sales of sheet music were easier to control. In the 1940s, the first associations for protecting the rights of the song-writers and publishers were formed; among the benefits songwriters received were royalties for each time a song they had written was recorded, performed, or played on the radio or in film.

By the 1950s, Tin Pan Alley no longer referred to a specific area in New York but was used nationwide to denote popular songs in general, and especially a type of simple melody and sentimental, often silly lyric that dominated the pop music industry. The rise of rock-and-roll music in the 1950s put an end to Tin Pan Alley's dom-inance. Many performers began to write their own songs, a trend that became particularly important in the 1960s. In the late 1970s, a new type of songwriting emerged. Rap music, featuring words chanted over a musical background, seemed to bring songwriting full circle, back to the oral traditions of its origins.

THE JOB

There are many different ways to write a song. A song may begin with a few words (the lyric) or with a few notes of a melody, or a song may be suggested by an idea, theme, or product. A song may come about in a flash of inspiration or may be developed slowly over a long period of time. Songwriters may work alone, or as part of a team, in which one person concentrates on the lyrics while another person concentrates on the music. Sometimes there may be several people working on the same song.

"One of the most important things," says songwriter Beth McBride, "is collecting your ideas, even if they're only fragments of ideas, and writing them down. Sometimes a song comes to me from beginning to end, but I can't always rely on inspiration. A lot of my writing has been personal, derived from experience and also from the observation of others' experiences." McBride performed for a decade with the band "B and the Hot Notes," for which she wrote and recorded original music. After she left the band, she focused on writ-ing and performing her own songs and released her first CD, *Recovering Grace,* in 2000.

Most popular songs require words, or lyrics, and some songwrit-ers may concentrate on writing the words to a song. These song-writers are called *lyricists.* Events, experiences, or emotions may inspire a lyricist to write lyrics. A lyricist may also be contracted to write the words for a jingle or musical, or to adapt the words from an existing song for another project.

Some songwriters do no more than write the words to a poten-tial song, leaving it to others to develop a melody and musical accompaniment for the words. They may sell the words to a music publisher or work in a team to create a finished song from the lyric. Some lyricists specialize in writing the words for advertising jingles. They are usually employed by advertising agencies and may work on several different products at once, often under pressure of a deadline.

In songwriting teams, one member may be a lyricist, while the other member is a composer. The development of a song can be a highly collaborative process. The composer might suggest topics for the song to the lyricist; the lyricist might suggest a melody to the composer. Other times, the composer plays a musical piece for the lyricist and the lyricist tries to create lyrics to fit that piece.

Composers for popular music generally have a strong background in music, and often in performing music as well. They must have an understanding of many musical styles, so that they can develop the music that will fit a project's needs. Composers work with a variety of musical and electronic equipment, including computers, to produce and record their music. They develop the different parts for the different musical instruments needed to play the song. They also work with musicians who will play and record the song, and the composer conducts or otherwise directs the musicians as the song is played.

Songwriters, composers, and musicians often make use of MIDI (musical instrument digital interface) technology to produce sounds through synthesizers, drum machines, and samplers. These sounds are usually controlled by a computer, and the composer or songwriter can mix, alter, and refine the sounds using mixing boards and computer software. Like analog or acoustic instruments, which produce sounds as a string, reed or drum head vibrates with air, MIDI creates digital "vibrations" that can produce sounds similar to acoustic instruments or highly unusual sounds invented by the songwriter. Synthesizers and other sound-producing machines may each have their own keyboard or playing mechanism, or be linked through one or more keyboards. They may also be controlled through the computer, or with other types of controls, such as a guitar controller, which plays like a guitar, or foot controls. Songs can be stored in the computer, or transferred to tape or compact disc.

Many, if not most, songwriters combine both the work of a lyricist and the work of a composer. Often, a songwriter will perform his or her own songs as well, whether as a singer, a member of a band, or both. Playing guitar has helped McBride in the writing of lyrics and music. "My songwriting has become more sophisticated as my playing has become more sophisticated," she says.

For most songwriters, writing a song is only the first part of their job. After a song is written, songwriters usually produce a "demo" of the song, so that the client or potential purchaser of the song can hear how it sounds. Songwriters contract with recording studios, studio musicians, and recording engineers to produce a version of the song. The songwriter then submits the song to a publishing house, record company, recording artist, film studio, or others, who will then decide if the song is appropriate for their needs. Often, a songwriter

Books about Songwriting

Austin, Dave, Mary Ellen Bickford, and Jim Peterik. *Songwriting For Dummies*. Hoboken, N.J.: John Wiley & Sons, 2002.

Bessler, Ian. *2004 Songwriter's Market: 1700 + Places to Market Your Songs*. Cincinnati, Ohio: Writers Digest Books, 2003.

Blume, Jason. *6 Steps to Songwriting Success: Comprehensive Guide to Writing and Marketing Hit Songs*. New York: Watson-Guptill, 1999.

Blume, Jason. *Inside Songwriting: Getting to the Heart of Creativity*. New York: Watson-Guptill, 2003.

Braheny, John. *The Craft and Business of Songwriting*. 2nd ed. Cincinnati, Ohio: Writers Digest Books, 2001.

Kachulis, Jimmy. *The Songwriter's Workshop: Melody*. Boston: Berklee Press Publications, 2003.

Leikin, Molly-Ann. *How to Be a Hit Songwriter: Polishing and Marketing Your Lyrics and Music*. Milwaukee, Wis.: Hal Leonard Corporation, 2003.

Luboff, Pat. *88 Songwriting Wrongs & How to Right Them: Concrete Ways to Improve Your Songwriting and Make Your Songs More Marketable*. Cincinnati, Ohio: Writers Digest Books, 1994.

Mitchell, Kevin M. *Essential Songwriters Rhyming Dictionary*. Van Nuys, Calif.: Alfred Publishing Company, 1996.

Weissman, Dick. *Songwriting: The Words, the Music and the Money*. Milwaukee, Wis.: Hal Leonard Corporation, 2001.

Zollo, Paul. *Songwriters on Songwriting*. Cambridge, Mass.: Da Capo Press, 2003.

will produce several versions of a song or submit several different songs for a particular project. There is always a chance that one, some, or all of their songs will be rejected.

REQUIREMENTS

High School

You should take courses that involve singing, playing instruments, and studying the history of music. Theater and speech classes will help you to understand the nature of performing, as well as involve you in writing dramatic pieces. You should study poetry in an English class, and try your hand at composing poetry in different forms. Language skills can also be honed in foreign-language classes and by working on student literary magazines. An understanding of how people act and think can influence you as a lyricist, so take courses in psychology and sociology.

Postsecondary Training

There are no real requirements for entering the field of songwriting. All songwriters, however, will benefit from musical training, including musical theory and musical notation. Learning to play one or more instruments, such as the piano or guitar, will be especially helpful in writing songs. Not all songwriters need to be able to sing, but this is helpful.

Songwriting is an extremely competitive field. Despite a lack of formal educational requirements, prospective songwriters are encouraged to continue their education through high school and, preferably, college. Much of the musical training a songwriter needs, however, can also be learned informally. In general, you should have a background in music theory and in arrangement and orchestration for multiple instruments. You should be able to read music, and be able to write it in the proper musical notation. You should have a good sense of the sounds each type of musical instrument produces, alone and in combination. Understanding harmony is important, as well as a proficiency in or understanding of a variety of styles of music. For example, you should know what makes rock different from reggae, blues, or jazz. Studies in music history will also help develop this understanding.

On the technical side, you should understand the various features, capabilities, and requirements of modern recording techniques. You should be familiar with MIDI and computer technology, as these play important roles in composing, playing, and recording music today.

There are several organizations that help lyricists, songwriters, and composers. The Songwriters Guild of America (http://www.songwriters.org) offers weekly song evaluation workshops in select cities. The Nashville Songwriters Association (http://www.nashvillesongwriters.com) offers workshops, seminars, and other services, as well as giving annual awards to songwriters. The Songwriters and Lyricists Club (P.O. Box 023304, Brooklyn, NY 11202) provides contacts for songwriters with music-business professionals. These and other organizations offer songwriting workshops and other training seminars.

Other Requirements

Many elements of songwriting cannot really be learned but are a matter of inborn talent. A creative imagination and the ability to invent melodies and combine melodies into a song are essential parts of a songwriting career. As you become more familiar with your own talents, and with songwriting, you'll learn to develop and enhance your creative skills.

"I enjoy observing," Beth McBride says. "I also enjoy the challenge of finding the most succinct way of saying something and making it poetic. I enjoy the process of finding that perfect turn of phrase. I really love language and words."

EXPLORING

The simplest way to gain experience in songwriting is to learn to play a musical instrument, especially the piano or guitar, and to invent your own songs. Joining a rock group is a way to gain experience writing music for several musicians. Most schools and communities have orchestras, bands, and choruses that are open to performers. Working on a student-written musical show is ideal training if you want to be a songwriter.

If you have your own computer, think about investing in software, a keyboard, and other devices that will allow you to experiment with sounds, recording, and writing and composing your own songs. While much of this equipment is expensive, there are plenty of affordable keyboards, drum machines, and software programs available today. Your school's music department may also have such equipment available.

EMPLOYERS

Most songwriters work freelance, competing for contracts to write songs for a particular artist, television show, video program, or for contracts with musical publishers and advertising agencies. They meet with clients to determine the nature of the project and to get an idea of what kind of music the client seeks, the budget for the project, the time in which the project should be completed, and in what form the work is to be submitted. Many songwriters work under contract with one or more music publishing houses. Usually, they must fulfill a certain quota of new songs each year. These songwriters receive a salary, called an advance or draw, that is often paid by the week. Once a song has been published, the money earned from the song goes to pay back the songwriter's draw. A percentage of the money earned by the song over and above the amount of the draw goes to the songwriter as a royalty. Other songwriters are employed by so-called "jingle houses," that is, companies that supply music for advertising commercials. Whereas most songwriters work in their own homes or offices, these songwriters work at the jingle house's offices. Film, television, and video production studios may also employ songwriters on their staff.

STARTING OUT

Songwriting is a very competitive career and difficult to break into for a beginner. The number of high-paying projects is limited. Often, beginning songwriters start their careers writing music for themselves or as part of a musical group. They may also offer their services to student films, student and local theater productions, church groups, and other religious and nonprofit organizations, often for free or for a low fee.

Many songwriters get their start while performing their own music in clubs and other venues; they may be approached by a music publisher, who contracts them for a number of songs. Other songwriters record demos of their songs and try to interest record companies and music publishers. Some songwriters organize showcase performances, renting a local club or hall and inviting music industry people to hear their work. Songwriters may have to approach many companies and publishers before they find one willing to buy their songs. Success in songwriting often comes through developing contacts with people active in the music industry.

Some songwriters get their start in one of the few entry-level positions available. Songwriters aspiring to become composers for film and television can find work as orchestrators or copyists in film houses. Other songwriters may find work for music agents and publishers, which will give them an understanding of the industry and increase their contacts in the business, as they develop their songwriting skills. Those interested in specializing in advertising jingles may find entry-level work as music production assistants with a jingle house. At first, such jobs may involve making coffee, doing paperwork, and completing other clerical tasks. As you gain more exposure to the process of creating music, you may begin in basic areas of music production, or assist experienced songwriters.

ADVANCEMENT

It is important for a songwriter to develop a strong portfolio of work and a reputation for professionalism. Songwriters who establish a reputation for producing quality work will receive larger and higher paying projects as their careers progress. They may be contracted to score major motion pictures, or to write songs for major recording artists. Ultimately, they may be able to support themselves on their songwriting alone and also have the ability to pick and choose the projects they will work on.

To continue to grow with the music industry, songwriters must be tuned into new musical styles and trends. They must also keep up with developments in music technology. A great deal of time is spent making and maintaining contacts with others in the music industry.

Songwriters specializing in jingles and other commercial products may eventually start up their own jingle house. Other songwriters, especially those who have written a number of hit songs, may themselves become recording artists.

For many songwriters, however, success and advancement is a very personal process. A confidence in your own talent will help you to create better work. "I'm not as vulnerable about my work," Beth McBride says. "And I want to open up my subject matter, to expand and experiment more."

EARNINGS

Songwriters' earnings vary widely, from next to nothing to many millions of dollars. A beginning songwriter may work for free, or for low pay, just to gain experience. A songwriter may sell a jingle to an advertising agency for $1,000 or may receive many thousands of dollars if his or her work is well known. Royalties from a song may reach $20,000 per year or more per song, and a successful songwriter may earn $100,000 or more per year from the royalties of several songs. A songwriter's earnings may come from a combination of royalties earned on songs and fees earned from commercial projects.

Those starting as assistants in music production companies or jingle houses may earn as little as $20,000 per year. Experienced songwriters at these companies may earn $50,000 per year or more.

Because most songwriters are freelance, they will have to provide their own health insurance, life insurance, and pension plans. They are usually paid per project, and therefore receive no overtime pay. When facing a deadline, they may have to work many more hours than eight hours a day or 40 hours a week. Also, songwriters are generally responsible for recording their own demos and must pay for recording studio time, studio musicians, and production expenses.

WORK ENVIRONMENT

Songwriters generally possess a strong love for music, and regardless of the level of their success, usually find fulfillment in their careers because they are doing what they love to do. As freelancers, they will control how they spend their day. They will work out of their own home or office. They will have their own instruments, and possibly their own recording equipment as well. Songwriters may also work in recording studios, where conditions can vary, from noisy and busy, to relaxed and quiet.

Writing music can be stressful. When facing a deadline, songwriters may experience a great deal of pressure while trying to get their music done just right and on time. They may face a great deal of rejection before they find someone willing to publish or record their songs. Rejection remains a part of the songwriter's life, even after success.

Many songwriters work many years with limited or no success. On the other hand, songwriters experience the joys of creativity, which has its own rewards.

OUTLOOK

Most songwriters are unable to support themselves from their songwriting alone and must hold other part-time or full-time jobs while writing songs in their spare time. The music industry is very competitive, and there are many more songwriters than paying projects. This situation is expected to continue into the next decade.

There are a few bright spots for songwriters. The recent rise of independent filmmaking has created more venues for songwriters to compose film scores. Cable television also provides more opportunities for song writing, both in the increased number of advertisements and in the growing trend for cable networks to develop original programs. Many computer games and software feature songs and music, and this area should grow rapidly in the next decade. Another boom area is the World Wide Web. As more and more companies, organizations, and individuals set up multimedia websites, there will be an increased demand for songwriters to create songs and music for these sites. Songwriters with MIDI capability will be in the strongest position to benefit from the growth created by computer uses of music. In another field, as legalized gambling has spread to many states in the country, a large number of resorts and theme parks have opened that produce their own musical theater and shows; they will require more songwriters.

Success in songwriting is a combination of hard work, industry connections, and good luck. The number of hit songs is very small compared to the number of songwriters trying to write them.

FOR MORE INFORMATION

For membership information, contact
American Society of Composers, Authors, and Publishers
One Lincoln Plaza
New York, NY 10023
Tel: 212-621-6000
http://www.ascap.com

Visit the Songwriter's section of the BMI website to learn more about performing rights, music publishing, copyright, and the business of songwriting.
Broadcast Music Inc. (BMI)
320 West 57th Street
New York, NY 10019
Tel: 212-586-2000
http://www.bmi.com

To learn about the annual young composer's competition and other contests, contact
National Association of Composers, USA
PO Box 49256, Barrington Station
Los Angeles, CA 90049
Tel: 310-541-8213
http://www.music-usa.org/nacusa

The SGA offers song critiques and other workshops in select cities. Visit its website for further information on such events.
Songwriters Guild of America (SGA)
1500 Harbor Boulevard
Weehawken, NJ 07086
Tel: 201-867-7603
http://www.songwriters.org

Index